The Presidency

Recent Titles in Student Guides to American Government and Politics

The Supreme Court
Helena Silverstein

The Presidency

Lori Cox Han

Student Guides to American Government and Politics
Brian Lloyd Fife, Series Editor

 GREENWOOD

An Imprint of ABC-CLIO, LLC
Santa Barbara, California • Denver, Colorado

Copyright © 2021 by ABC-CLIO, LLC

Library of Congress Cataloging-in-Publication Data

Names: Han, Lori Cox, author.
Title: The presidency / Lori Cox Han.
Description: Santa Barbara, California : Greenwood, an Imprint of ABC-CLIO,
    2021. | Series: Student guides to American government and politics |
    Includes bibliographical references and index.
Identifiers: LCCN 2020035099 (print) | LCCN 2020035100 (ebook) | ISBN
    9781440873942 (hardcover) | ISBN 9781440873959 (ebook)
Subjects: LCSH: Presidents—United States. | Executive power—United
    States. | Political leadership—United States. | United States—Politics
    and government.
Classification: LCC JK516 .H249 2021 (print) | LCC JK516 (ebook) | DDC
    352.230973--dc23
LC record available at https://lccn.loc.gov/2020035099
LC ebook record available at https://lccn.loc.gov/2020035100

ISBN: 978-1-4408-7394-2 (print)
        978-1-4408-7395-9 (ebook)

25 24 23 22 21   1 2 3 4 5

This book is also available as an eBook.

Greenwood
An Imprint of ABC-CLIO, LLC

ABC-CLIO, LLC
147 Castilian Drive
Santa Barbara, California 93117
www.abc-clio.com

This book is printed on acid-free paper ∞

Manufactured in the United States of America

Contents

Preface

The American presidency is one of the most unique and fascinating political positions ever created. With powers that are both vast and limited and responsibilities that are both constitutionally mandated and ceremonial or symbolic, those who have held the position and the office itself have been a constant source of observation and discussion for scholars, the American public, and media. The institutional features of the office serve as both a benefit and a burden to the occupants of the Oval Office, just as the individuals who have served as president bring different personal skills (or lack thereof) that shape the successes and failures of any administration. As presidential scholars Thomas E. Cronin and Michael Genovese argue in their book *The Paradoxes of the American Presidency* (1998), the American presidency is defined by many paradoxes that determine the potential for presidential leadership.

It is important to remember, however, that the presidency is but one part of the executive branch of government, which is in turn one of the three coequal branches within the American constitutional system. For anyone seeking a better understanding of the president's role within that system, the constitutional foundations of the office provide the best starting point. As such, the goal of this volume is to provide a brief yet thorough explanation of the office of the presidency, including its role within the constitutional system of government, the powers of the office (both enumerated and inherent or implied), and how individual presidents have shaped the office since George Washington became the nation's first president in 1789.

In the chapters that follow, these core topics will be considered to analyze specific areas relevant to the constitutional and political responsibilities of American presidents. The introduction provides a brief overview of the office and the individuals who have held it, as well as the different historical eras and the many resources on which scholars of the presidency rely on studying this important topic. Chapter 1 lays out the powers of the presidency as found within the U.S. Constitution and explains the difference between enumerated and inherent/implied powers. Major decisions by the U.S. Supreme Court regarding presidential powers are also discussed. Chapter 2 considers the presidential selection process and describes the three phases of a presidential campaign: the pre-nomination phase, the nomination phase, and the general election. Chapter 3 looks at the public aspects of the presidency, including White House communication strategies, the president's relationship with the news media, and public opinion. Chapters 4, 5, and 6 provide an analysis of the president's relationship with the three branches of government—Congress, the judiciary, and the executive branch. Chapter 7 considers the president's role in the policymaking process regarding domestic, economic, and foreign matters. The concluding chapter considers the future of the office of the presidency and the role it will continue to play in the American governing process. Throughout the book, individual presidents provide many fascinating examples of the various challenges that exist when it comes to seeking the office of the presidency as well as in attempting to govern a nation that is vast in geographic size and home to a multitude of industries, ethnicities, cultures, faiths, and political convictions.

Acknowledgments

Every book project, no matter how big or small, brings together the work of many individuals beyond just the author. In this case, I have been fortunate to work again with my editor at ABC-CLIO, Kevin Hillstrom, whose contributions have been invaluable. His knowledge of the publishing process, enthusiasm for all scholarly aspects of the American presidency, and most importantly, his support and patience while I worked through the manuscript are deeply appreciated. I also thank the editor of the Student Guides to American Government and Politics series, Brian Fife, for including me in this important set of reference works. I hope that my work here provides a small contribution in our efforts to expand civic knowledge far and wide. I have many others to thank for their never-ending encouragement and support, most notably my "team" at Chapman University. At the top of that list is Talisa Flores, administrative assistant in the Political Science Department, who helps to keep me organized. I remain deeply grateful for the support that I receive for my research endeavors from President Daniele Struppa, Provost Glenn Pfeiffer, and Jennifer Keene, dean of Wilkinson College of Arts, Humanities, and Social Sciences. Last, but certainly not least, my husband, Tom Han, and children, Taylor NyBlom and Davis Han, are the three people who keep me focused and grounded, and for that, I am beyond blessed.

Introduction

Imagine that you were tasked with explaining the American presidency to someone who knew literally nothing about the system of government in the United States. Where would you begin and what words would you use to describe both the office of the presidency and those who have held the position? While it may seem as if American presidents have tremendous power—often described as the most powerful position in the world—the reality is that despite the many perks of the job and the many trappings of the office, presidents are often at the mercy of other political actors when attempting to govern. The president may be the top official of the executive branch of government, but it is one of three coequal branches within the American constitutional system of government thanks to the framers' belief in separation of powers and checks and balances. And while presidential campaigns are media-dominated affairs that focus on image, sound bites, and messaging skills of the candidates (not to mention the personalities of those seeking the highest office in the land), the ability to effectively govern is a much different proposition than attracting voters on the campaign trail. In a nutshell, the American presidency is often more complicated and nuanced than a casual observer might surmise.

In addition, while many nations around the globe seek to emulate ideals associated with the American system of government, such as voting rights and free speech (to name just a few), few nations have modeled the American presidency, not to mention the process by which presidents are selected. Several features, including the president's role as commander in chief, the dual role of head of state and head of government, and the size and scope of the executive branch that the president oversees, make the American presidency unique.

In the chapters that follow, we will explore the many constitutional, institutional, and political features of the American presidency, including the powers of the office, the presidential selection process, the president's relationship with other political actors, and the policymaking process. But first, let's begin with a brief overview of key facts and features of the American presidency to better understand the political context in which this unique political position operates.

PRESIDENTIAL DEMOGRAPHICS

A total of 46 men have held the office of the presidency. Joseph R. Biden became the 46th president when he took the oath of office on January 20, 2021; Grover Cleveland served two non-consecutive terms as president (1885–1889, 1893–1897), so he is counted twice. Elected in 2016, Donald J. Trump is unique in that he became the first president in U.S. history elected with no prior political or military experience. Prior to Trump's election, Dwight Eisenhower (1953–1961) was the only president ever elected with no previous political experience.

Many demographic trends emerge when considering the 46 men who have been president. Similarities exist in some areas, while little diversity exists in others. Here are some of the most common categories used when looking at the facts and figures associated with the American presidency:

Age: The average age of presidents on the day of their inauguration is approximately 55 years old. Biden is the oldest candidate elected president; he was 78 when he took the oath of office. Trump was 70 when he took office in 2017, which was roughly six months older than Ronald Reagan when he took office in 1981. The youngest president to serve was Theodore Roosevelt at age 42 (he became president upon the assassination of William McKinley in 1901), while the youngest president ever elected was John F. Kennedy at age 43 (he was also the youngest to die in office; he was 46 when he was assassinated in 1963).

State Residency: Presidents hail from a total of 18 states, with seven each from New York and Ohio, five from Virginia, and four from Massachusetts.

Race/Ethnicity: The families of 40 presidents originated from Great Britain (England, Scotland, Ireland), while three came from the Netherlands (Theodore Roosevelt, Franklin D. Roosevelt, and Martin Van Buren), one from Germany (Dwight Eisenhower), and one from Africa (Barack Obama is biracial; his father was Kenyan).

Religion: A majority of presidents (36) were Protestant, while seven were nontrinitarian or had no official affiliation. To date, John F. Kennedy and Biden are the only Catholic presidents. Among those who were Protestant, 11 were Episcopalian and eight were Presbyterian.

Marriage and Family: Only one president, James Buchanan, never married. Only two presidents have been divorced (Donald Trump twice and Ronald Reagan once), and five presidents had no children (George

Washington, Andrew Jackson, James Buchanan, James K. Polk, and Warren Harding).

College Education: Most presidents have had college degrees; only 12 never attended college or never graduated. The last president to hold no college degree was Harry S. Truman (though he did complete some college courses). Five presidents had undergraduate degrees from Harvard, including John Adams, John Quincy Adams, Theodore Roosevelt, Franklin D. Roosevelt, and John F. Kennedy. Seven presidents had law degrees (both Roosevelts, Richard Nixon, Gerald Ford, Bill Clinton, and Barack Obama), and George W. Bush is the only president to hold an MBA. Woodrow Wilson is the only president to have earned a PhD (in political science from Johns Hopkins University).

Previous Job: The most common previous job held by presidents has been either state governorship (16 total; four of the last seven presidents were state governors—George W. Bush of Texas, Bill Clinton of Arkansas, Ronald Reagan of California, and Jimmy Carter of Georgia) or membership in the U.S. Senate (16 total; Barack Obama, who represented Illinois, was the most recent). All but 13 presidents had prior military experience, including 11 who served as general (the most notable being Dwight Eisenhower, who was a five-star general in the army and served as Supreme Commander of the Allied Expeditionary Force in Europe during World War II). The most recent presidents with no military experience are Joseph R. Biden, Donald J. Trump, Barack Obama, and Bill Clinton.

Death in Office: Four presidents have been assassinated (Abraham Lincoln in 1865, James Garfield in 1881, William McKinley in 1901, and John F. Kennedy in 1963). Four other presidents died of natural causes while in office (William Henry Harrison in 1841, Zachary Taylor in 1850, Warren G. Harding in 1923, and Franklin D. Roosevelt in 1945).

Impeachment: Three presidents have been impeached by the House of Representatives—Andrew Johnson in 1868, Bill Clinton in 1998, and Donald J. Trump in 2019 and 2021. All were acquitted in their Senate trials, so no president has ever been removed from office. In 1974, Richard Nixon resigned from office (the only president to ever do so) prior to a vote of impeachment in the House (though the House Judiciary Committee had approved articles of impeachment).

Vice Presidents: Forty-eight men and one woman have held the position of vice president; 15 went on to become president themselves, with nine succeeding to the position due to presidential death or resignation.

Gender: No women has yet to be elected president. Only one woman to date has received a major party nomination for president (Democrat Hillary Clinton in 2016), and three have been nominated for vice president (Democrats Geraldine Ferraro in 1984, Kamala Harris in 2020, and Republican Sarah Palin in 2008). Harris became the first woman vice president in 2021.

PRESIDENTIAL ERAS

As a political institution, the American presidency represents an excellent case study of the powers and intricacies of the office. While the occupant of the White House changes every few years, only minor changes have been adopted to the constitutional structure of the office since it was first created in 1789. However, the presidency of the eighteenth century seems weak in comparison to the powers that are now associated with the twenty-first century presidency. And while some presidents are considered great leaders (such as Abraham Lincoln or Franklin D. Roosevelt), others were mostly forgettable (such as William Henry Harrison, who served only 31 days before dying in office in 1841). The U.S. Constitution, along with the political institutions outlined within it, has proven to be amazingly resilient by enduring numerous wars (including the Civil War from 1861 to 1865), scandals (such as Watergate, which led to Richard Nixon's resignation from office in 1974), economic turbulence (such as the Great Depression following the stock market crash in 1929), and even four presidential assassinations. The political circumstances and environments for each president have varied over time, as have the skill sets that each president has brought to the Oval Office. In general, though, scholars of the presidency often divide the history of the office into three principal eras: the traditional presidency, the modern presidency, and the postmodern or contemporary presidency.

The traditional presidency includes presidents from the late eighteenth century until the turn of the twentieth century. With a few notable exceptions, most of these men were not particularly memorable. During this era, as difficult as it may be to believe, being president was not considered a top political prize within the American system of government. Many of the early presidents never aspired to the position, as it offered little prestige or authority over the policymaking process. This is due, in part, to the fact that the United States at that time was not a major player in global affairs; the power associated with the president's role as commander in chief and diplomat regarding foreign relations would not emerge until the twentieth century. Governors in some of the larger states during the late eighteenth and early nineteenth centuries, such as New York, Massachusetts, and Virginia, actually had more powerful political positions than did the president. A weaker presidency than what we see today is what the framers of the Constitution had intended. As a result, presidents during this era merely carried out the laws passed by Congress, which assumed the role of the dominant policymaking branch.

Nonetheless, four presidents from the traditional era stand out: George Washington (1789–1797), Thomas Jefferson (1801–1809), Andrew Jackson (1829–1837), and Abraham Lincoln (1861–1865), all of whom provided bold and decisive leadership that helped to set precedents for the office as well as expand presidential authority. Washington, as the first to hold the office, set many precedents and shaped the model of presidential leadership for generations to come. Jefferson, as the author of the Declaration of Independence and one of the most prominent among the founding generation (although he is not considered a "framer" of the Constitution as he was not present at the constitutional convention in 1787), is remembered for articulating his beliefs in republicanism and a limited national government. Yet, he pushed the constitutional limits of presidential powers with his decision to use military force against the Barbary Pirates in 1801 and purchase the Louisiana Territory in 1803 without consulting Congress on either decision. Jackson became the first "common man" to hold the presidency. He rose to power during a time when both grassroots politics and political parties became prominent electoral fixtures and voting rights expanded beyond land-owning elites. Lincoln, considered by some scholars and many Americans as the greatest president, held the nation together during the Civil War. Yet he is also known for expanding presidential powers by relying on extraconstitutional or unconstitutional measures in doing so (including the suspension of habeas corpus, which is a fundamental right within the Constitution that protects citizens against unlawful or indefinite imprisonment).

While some scholars debate when the "modern" presidency began, it is generally accepted that the turn of the twentieth century ushered in an era in which both presidential powers and presidential leadership expanded beyond the mostly limited examples that occurred since 1789. Beginning with Theodore Roosevelt's presidency that began with William McKinley's assassination in 1901 and ended in early 1909, presidents became more active in shaping the national agenda, waging wars, and connecting with the American public. Roosevelt is often associated with what is known as the stewardship theory, which means that he saw the president as the "steward" of the American people and assumed that the office held expansive powers as long as the Constitution was not violated. At the same time that the powers associated with the presidency began to expand, so too did the size of the executive branch of government, as agencies needed to be created or expanded to help the president carry out his initiatives and policies. According to presidential scholar Louis Koenig, Theodore Roosevelt and Woodrow Wilson (who served as president from 1913 to 1921) were the modern presidency's "architects, as asserters of bold undertakings in domestic and foreign affairs, as gifted mobilizers of public opinion, as inducers of congressional concurrence."[1] Of the three branches, the executive branch has moved farthest from its origins and least resembles the intent of its framers.

With Franklin D. Roosevelt's election in 1932, the executive branch further expanded in both size and power. Roosevelt's three-plus terms in office (1933–1945, he died three months into his fourth term) saw several important changes that solidified the modern presidency: enhanced presidential staff resources, a greater presidential role in policymaking, a stronger relationship with the mass public, and a greater presence in fostering international relationships.[2] These changes occurred as Roosevelt enacted his New Deal initiatives to combat the Great Depression. Roosevelt's New Deal legislation gave tremendous political power to the federal government in regulating various aspects of the American economy (such as creating public works programs, regulating maximum hours in a work week, establishing minimum wages and working conditions, regulating banks and other financial institutions, and establishing Social Security benefits, just to name a few). In addition, when the United States entered World War II following the attack on Pearl Harbor by Japan in December 1941, the president's role as commander in chief expanded, as did the size and authority of the federal agencies associated with the American military response. By the mid-1940s, the power of the executive branch had eclipsed that of both the legislative and judicial branches of government.

In the aftermath of the Roosevelt presidency, both Harry S. Truman (1945–1953) and Dwight Eisenhower (1953–1961) continued to expand the powers of the office. During this same period, the United States' status as an economic and military global superpower and its "Cold War" with the Soviet Union dominated both domestic and foreign policymaking. The public aspects of the office, thanks to expanding media technology (especially television) as well as an increased expectation for strong presidential leadership among the public, also increased during the mid-twentieth century. By the time of John F. Kennedy's presidency (1961–1963), the use of television and other White House communication strategies became accepted as a way for presidents to communicate with and lead the American public.

As America's status as a global superpower became broadly accepted across the nation and around the world, presidents pursued extensive policy agendas both at home and abroad. Lyndon Johnson's (1963–1969) Great Society program included a War on Poverty and many other domestic programs that either expanded on New Deal programs or created new federal agencies and initiatives. Combatting the spread of communism (often called containment) became a major factor in U.S. foreign policy during this time. However, the failure of that policy during the protracted Vietnam War called into question the powers of the modern presidency. Critics labeled both Johnson and Richard Nixon (1969–1974) as "imperial" presidents for their actions in Vietnam (due in part to the fact that Congress never officially declared war during the conflict).[3]

Following Nixon's resignation from office in 1974 as a result of the Watergate scandal, and the end of the Vietnam War in 1975, the powers of the modern presidency diminished. Changes in the U.S. economy (including increasing budget deficits) as well as a loss of public trust in the executive branch shifted public expectations for presidential leadership. For some scholars, the American presidency had entered a new postmodern phase. By the 1980s, presidents found it more difficult to pursue big domestic political agendas; Ronald Reagan instead focused on deregulation and tax reduction as part of his domestic political agenda as opposed to creating new programs and policies. Divided government became more common (with the White House controlled by one political party and at least one house of Congress controlled by the other), and with fewer budgetary resources thanks to a spiraling national debt, the president had much less room to invest in ambitious federal programs. Instead, Ronald Reagan's (1981–1989) electoral success and popularity was based in part on his promise to reduce the size of the federal government. In addition, with the end of the Cold War at the close of the 1980s, presidents lost power in the international arena. The collapse of the Soviet Union was perceived as greatly lessening the threats of communism and nuclear war. Cooperation in what George H.W. Bush (1989–1993) called "the new world order" came to be seen in many quarters as the primary focus of American foreign policy.

While Bill Clinton (1993–2001) focused extensively on domestic and economic issues while in office, the terrorist attacks on September 11, 2001, pushed George W. Bush (2001–2009) to reassert presidential power with military actions in both Afghanistan and Iraq. These military deployments were based upon the belief that the United States must preempt and prevent potential threats to national security. This belief came to be known as the Bush Doctrine.

The debate over presidential powers in both economic and foreign policy arenas continued into the Barack Obama presidency (2009–2017). Upon taking office in January 2009, Obama inherited the Great Recession (which began in the United States in late 2007) as well as both wars in Afghanistan and Iraq. While economic conditions had improved by the start of the Trump presidency in 2017, his administration faced ongoing national security issues, as well as global economic and trade issues on various fronts (including relations with Russia, China, the Middle East, and North Korea, among others).

This postmodern or contemporary presidency is defined by several factors, including the way in which Americans select their presidents; the political skills necessary for a candidate to succeed on the campaign trail are different from those needed to handle the complex domestic, economic, and global demands of the job. The challenges faced by recent presidents represent both the increased powers and diminished capacities of governing that have evolved in recent decades. In addition, presidents must now contend with a political environment dominated by hyper-partisanship.

This partisanship is fueled by nonstop media coverage that for many outlets requires partisan or sensational news coverage to make a profit.

STUDYING THE AMERICAN PRESIDENCY

Regardless of fluctuations in the power and influence presidents possess over the policymaking process, they still represent one of the most studied aspects of American government. Compared to Congress, with 535 members and a complicated system of committees and subcommittees that dominate the policymaking process, or the nine members of the U.S. Supreme Court, who serve for life terms and do not need to campaign for office or worry about public opinion for reelection, the president is a single individual who symbolizes the U.S. government (especially on the world stage). As a result, the president receives more media attention than any other political actor and so does the personal aspects of the president's life. Americans have a long history of admiring the office of the presidency—although they have not always admired the individual who holds the office.

For those scholars who study the presidency, various methods and sources exist. Some scholars study the institution of the presidency or the executive branch of government. This is most often referred to as a presidency-centered approach. Other scholars focus instead on a president-centered approach, studying various traits, skills, and strategies of individual presidents. Most books and articles published on presidents and the presidency come from political scientists, historians, or journalists. In recent years, presidential scholarship has embraced a variety of theories and methodologies: some more qualitative (for example, a case study approach to understand a president's actions regarding a specific policy initiative, such as Obama's pursuit of health care reform) and some more quantitative (for example, a statistical analysis of the use of executive orders across several administrations).

Several important resources exist for those who study the presidency, but two of the most important include the presidential library system and the *Public Papers of the Presidents of the United States*. The presidential library system, under the auspices of the National Archives and Records Administration (NARA), includes a total of 13 presidential libraries and museums (Herbert Hoover through George W. Bush). The newest addition will be the Barack Obama Presidential Center, set to open in 2021. However, unlike at the other presidential libraries, Obama's presidential papers will be digitized and the physical copies will not be made available to scholars.

In general, presidential libraries are repositories for the papers, records, and historical materials of the presidents, working to ensure that these irreplaceable items are preserved and made available for the widest possible use by researchers. According to NARA, the goal of presidential libraries is to "promote understanding of the presidency and the American experience" as well as to "preserve and provide access to historical materials, support research, and create interactive programs and exhibits that educate and inspire."

The working papers for each administration since Herbert Hoover are available in presidential libraries. The Library of Congress houses the papers for most administrations prior to Hoover. Presidential libraries are not normal libraries; rather, they are archives and museums that house the documents and artifacts of a president and his administration. Millions of visitors pass through presidential museums each year, while researchers and journalists can access documents from each administration. Numerous special events are held at these libraries. These are typically funded and sponsored by the president's private foundation (to help promote the legacy of each president as well as to provide financial support for educational programs). The library archives themselves are managed by NARA archivists, which ensures open access with no political or ideological affiliation. Each of the libraries is also associated with a museum. Gerald Ford's library and museum are the only ones not housed together (the library is at the University of Michigan in Ann Arbor, and the museum is 130 miles away in Grand Rapids, Michigan).

The presidential library system first began in 1939 with Franklin D. Roosevelt, who wanted to preserve the papers and other materials from his time in office. Prior to the precedent set by Roosevelt, papers were often dispersed to family members and administration officials, and many were even destroyed. In 1955, Congress passed the Presidential Libraries Act, which established a system of libraries to be built through private funds and then turned over to the federal government to maintain and oversee. Since that time, when a president leaves office, NARA establishes a Presidential Project until the new presidential library is built and transferred to the federal government.

In 1978, Congress passed the Presidential Records Act (PRA), which established that presidential records documenting the constitutional, statutory, and ceremonial duties of the president are the property of the United States Government. While the first presidential libraries built acknowledged the fact that presidential papers were the personal property of the president, NARA had great success in persuading presidents to donate their historical materials to be housed in a NARA-run presidential library. However, Richard Nixon's resignation from office in 1974 triggered numerous lawsuits over ownership of his presidential papers, which in part encouraged Congress to change the law. Another provision of the PRA, signed into law by Jimmy Carter, stipulated that each presidential library established after Carter's would be governed by the Freedom of Information Act (FOIA), a law passed in 1966 to ensure public access to government documents of a non-classified nature.

Started in 1957, the *Public Papers of the Presidents of the United States* series is the official annual compilation of presidential papers. It provides a comprehensive public source of data on the American presidency. The *Public Papers* is now the annual version of the *Weekly Compilation of Presidential Documents*, which began publication in 1965. As of January 2009, the *Weekly Compilation* was replaced by the *Daily Compilation of Presidential Documents*. Both the *Public Papers* and the *Daily Compilation* are published by the Office of the Federal Register, National Archives and Records Service, and are printed by the Government Printing Office. Administrations included in the series of *Public Papers* include those of Herbert Hoover through Barack Obama, with one exception—the papers of Franklin Roosevelt were published privately prior to the creation of the official *Public Papers* series. The *Public Papers* include the papers and speeches of the President of the United States that were issued by the Office of the Press Secretary. Specifically, these include press releases, presidential proclamations, executive orders, addresses, remarks, letters, messages, telegrams, memorandums to federal agencies, communications to Congress, bill-signing statements, transcripts from presidential press conferences, and communiqués to foreign heads of state. The appendixes in each volume of the *Public Papers* are extensive and include listings of a digest of the president's daily schedule and meetings and other items issued by the White House press secretary; the president's nominations submitted to the Senate; a checklist of materials released by the Office of the Press Secretary that are not printed full-text in the book; and a table of Proclamations, Executive Orders, and other presidential documents released by the Office of the Press Secretary and published in the Federal Register. Each volume also includes a foreword signed by the president, several photographs chosen from White House Photo Office files, a subject and name index, and a document categories list. Electronic versions of the *Public Papers* can be found at the Government Publishing Office website as well as individual presidential library websites. In addition, The American Presidency Project (americanpresidency.org), established at the University of California, Santa Barbara, is an extensive online archive containing nearly 120,000 documents related to the study of the presidency. Donald Trump's use of Twitter has been a concern for archivists regarding preservation of this favored mode of presidential communication, though electronic correspondence is considered material that should be protected, and the Trump White House has stated they are complying with current presidential records laws.

CONCLUSION

The American presidency remains one of the most recognizable positions of power in the world, and the office and its occupants continue to be a great source of fascination and study for scholars as well as the public at large. Americans celebrate President's Day each February as a national holiday, and there is no shortage of presidential trivia or memorabilia available to those who are interested. Perhaps the most compelling feature of the office is how, thanks to the constitutional design of the office, presidents can be both powerful and weak in the actions they take. While much about the modern American political process is centered on the presidency, presidents have few unilateral powers at their disposal. It is from that perspective that we will take a closer look at all aspects of the presidency in the chapters that follow.

NOTES

1. Louis W. Koenig, *The Chief Executive*, 6th ed. (New York, NY: Harcourt Brace, 1996), 3.

2. Jeffrey Cohen and David Nice, *The Presidency* (New York, NY: McGraw-Hill, 2003), 53–59, and Sidney M. Milkis and Michael Nelson, *The American Presidency: Origins and Development, 1776–2014*, 7th ed. (Washington, DC: CQ Press, 2016), 301–304.

3. The term "imperial president" is most often associated with the book of the same title by historian Arthur Schlesinger, Jr., in which he discusses the modern presidency. See Schlesinger, *The Imperial Presidency* (Boston, MA: Houghton Mifflin Company, 1973).

REFERENCES

Cohen, Jeffrey, and David Nice. 2003. *The Presidency.* New York: McGraw-Hill.

Han, Lori Cox. and Diane J. Heith. 2018. *Presidents and the American Presidency*, 2nd ed. New York: Oxford University Press.

Koenig, Louis W. 1996. *The Chief Executive*, 6th ed. New York: Harcourt Brace.

Milkis, Sidney M., and Michael Nelson. 2016. *The American Presidency: Origins and Development, 1776–2014*, 7th ed. Washington, DC: CQ Press.

Pika, Joseph A., John Anthony Maltese, and Andrew Rudalevige. 2017. *The Politics of the Presidency*, 9th ed. Washington, DC: CQ Press.

Schlesinger, Arthur Schlesinger, Jr. 1973. *The Imperial Presidency.* Boston, MA: Houghton Mifflin Company.

Chronology

The following chronology highlights key events in the development and expansion of the presidency as an institution and identifies presidential elections and other notable events related to presidential powers and leadership.

1789
George Washington (Federalist) is elected the first president in a unanimous vote in the Electoral College. John Adams (Federalist) is elected vice president.

1792
President George Washington and Vice President John Adams are reelected.

1796
John Adams (Federalist) is elected president, and Thomas Jefferson (Democratic-Republican) is elected vice president.

1800
Thomas Jefferson (Democratic-Republican) is elected president, and Aaron Burr (Democratic-Republican) is elected vice president.

1804
President Thomas Jefferson is reelected, and George Clinton (Democratic-Republican) is elected vice president.

1808
James Madison (Democratic-Republican) is elected president. Vice president George Clinton (Democratic-Republican) is reelected.

1812
President James Madison is reelected, and Elbridge Gerry (Democratic-Republican) is elected vice president.

1816

James Monroe (Democratic-Republican) is elected president, and Daniel D. Tompkins (Democratic-Republican) is elected vice president.

1820

President James Monroe and Vice President Daniel D. Tompkins are reelected.

1824

John Quincy Adams (Democratic-Republican) is elected president, and John C. Calhoun (Democratic-Republican) is elected vice president.

1828

Andrew Jackson (Democratic) is elected president, and Vice President John C. Calhoun is reelected.

1832

President Andrew Jackson is reelected, and Martin Van Buren (Democratic) is elected vice president.

1835

President Andrew Jackson survives the first attempted presidential assassination when the assailant's gun misfires.

1836

Martin Van Burn (Democratic) is elected president, and Richard Johnson (Democratic) is elected vice president.

1840

William Henry Harrison (Whig) is elected president, and John Tyler (Whig) is elected vice president.

1841

President William Henry Harrison becomes the first president to die in office after serving for just 31 days (the shortest tenure to date). Vice President John Tyler succeeds to the presidency.

1844

James K. Polk (Democratic) is elected president, and George M. Dallas (Democratic) is elected vice president.

1848

Zachary Taylor (Whig) is elected president, and Millard Fillmore (Whig) is elected vice president.

1850

President Zachary Taylor dies in office, and Vice President Millard Fillmore succeeds to the presidency.

1852

Franklin Pierce (Democratic) is elected president, and William R. King (Democratic) is elected vice president.

1856

James Buchanan (Democratic) is elected president, and John C. Breckenridge (Democratic) is elected vice president.

1860

Abraham Lincoln (Republican) is elected president, and Hannibal Hamlin (Republican) is elected vice president.

1861

The U.S. Civil War begins when Confederate forces open fire on Fort Sumter in South Carolina.

1864

President Abraham Lincoln is reelected, and Andrew Johnson (Democrat) is elected vice president.

1865

President Abraham Lincoln is assassinated by John Wilkes Booth (an actor and Confederate sympathizer) in April, the first president to die by an assassin's bullet. Vice President Andrew Johnson succeeds to the presidency.

The U.S. Civil War ends in May following the surrender by the Confederate Army in April.

1868

President Andrew Johnson becomes the first president to be impeached by the House of Representatives for violating the Tenure of Office Act. He is acquitted in the U.S. Senate.

Ulysses S. Grant (Republican) is elected president, and Schuyler Colfax (Republican) is elected vice president.

1872

President Ulysses S. Grant is reelected, and Henry Wilson (Republican) is elected vice president.

1876

Rutherford B. Hayes (Republican) is elected president, and William Wheeler (Republican) is elected vice president.

1880

James A. Garfield (Republican) is elected president, and Chester A. Arthur (Republican) is elected vice president.

1881

President James A. Garfield is assassinated; he is shot by Charles Guiteau (who believes Garfield owes him a political appointment) in July and dies two months later. Vice President Chester A. Arthur succeeds to the presidency.

1884

Grover Cleveland (Democratic) is elected president, and Thomas Hendricks (Democratic) is elected vice president.

1888

Benjamin Harrison (Republican) is elected president, and Levi Morton (Republican) is elected vice president.

1892

Grover Cleveland (Democratic) is elected president, and Adlai Stevenson (Democratic) is elected vice president.

1896

William McKinley (Republican) is elected president, and Garret Hobart (Republican) is elected vice president.

1900

President William McKinley is reelected, and Theodore Roosevelt (Republican) is elected vice president.

1901

President William McKinley is assassinated in September in Buffalo, New York, by anarchist Leon Czolgosz. Vice President Theodore Roosevelt succeeds to the presidency.

1904

President Theodore Roosevelt is reelected, and Charles W. Fairbanks (Republican) is elected vice president.

1908

William Howard Taft (Republican) is elected president, and James S. Sherman (Republican) is elected vice president.

1912

Woodrow Wilson (Democratic) is elected president, and Thomas R. Marshall (Democratic) is elected vice president.

1916

President Woodrow Wilson and Vice President Thomas R. Marshall are reelected.

1917

The U.S. declares war on Germany and enters World War I, with nearly four million troops serving in Europe prior to its end.

1918
World War I ends with the signing of the Armistice of 11 November 1918.

1920
Warren G. Harding (Republican) is elected president, and Calvin Coolidge (Republican) is elected vice president.

1923
President Warren G. Harding dies of heart failure in August in San Francisco while touring the nation. Vice President Calvin Coolidge succeeds to the presidency.

1924
President Calvin Coolidge is reelected, and Charles G. Dawes (Republican) is elected vice president.

1928
Herbert Hoover (Republican) is elected president, and Charles Curtis (Republican) is elected vice president.

1929
Stock market crash in October triggers a cascade of events that result in the economic collapse known as the Great Depression.

1932
Franklin D. Roosevelt (Democratic) is elected president, and John Nance Garner (Democratic) is elected vice president. Upon entering the White House, Roosevelt launches an ambitious series of programs and policies collectively known as the New Deal to combat the Depression.

1933
The Twentieth Amendment is ratified, which changes the date on which the terms of the president and vice president begin from March 4 to January 20. In addition, if the president-elect dies, is not chosen, or is deemed ineligible prior to inauguration, then the vice president-elect is inaugurated as president in their place.

1936
President Franklin D. Roosevelt and Vice President John Nance Garner are reelected.

1940
President Franklin D. Roosevelt is reelected, and Henry A. Wallace (Democratic) is elected vice president.

1941
The United States enters World War II after the bombing of Pearl Harbor on December 7; war is declared on Japan, Germany, and the Axis allies.

1944

President Franklin D. Roosevelt is reelected, and Harry S. Truman (Democratic) is elected vice president.

1945

President Franklin D. Roosevelt dies of a massive brain hemorrhage in Warm Spring, Georgia, in April, just three months into his fourth term in office. Vice President Harry S. Truman succeeds to the presidency.

World War II ends with Nazi Germany's surrender in May and Japan's surrender in August. Days prior to Japan's surrender, President Harry S. Truman orders atomic bombs to be dropped on the cities of Hiroshima and Nagasaki.

1948

President Harry S. Truman is reelected, and Alben W. Barkley (Democratic) is elected vice president.

1950

The Korean War begins in June when North Korea invades South Korea. The United Nations, with mostly U.S. troops, supports South Korea while China and the Soviet Union support the communist government in North Korea.

Pro-Puerto Rican independence activists attempt to assassinate President Harry S. Truman in Washington, D.C. in November.

1951

The Twenty-Second Amendment is ratified, which limits the president to two terms. In addition, the amendment stipulates that someone who succeeds to the presidency and serves more than two years for someone else who has been elected cannot serve more than one term beyond that time.

1952

Dwight D. Eisenhower (Republican) is elected president, and Richard M. Nixon (Republican) is elected vice president.

1953

The Korean War ends in July with the signing of the Korean Armistice Agreement, which ends all hostilities between the North and South but which ends the war in a stalemate.

1956

President Dwight D. Eisenhower and Vice President Richard M. Nixon are reelected.

1960

John F. Kennedy (Democratic) is elected president, and Lyndon B. Johnson (Democratic) is elected vice president.

1961

The Twenty-Third Amendment is ratified, which grants the District of Columbia three votes in the Electoral College.

1963

President John F. Kennedy is assassinated in Dallas, Texas, on November 22 by Lee Harvey Oswald, a communist sympathizer. Vice President Lyndon B. Johnson succeeds to the presidency.

1964

President Lyndon B. Johnson is reelected, and Hubert H. Humphrey (Democratic) is elected vice president.

1965

The United States sends the first American ground troops to Vietnam.

1967

The Twenty-Fifth Amendment is ratified. It addresses succession to the presidency by establishing a procedure to fill a vacancy in the vice presidency. In addition, procedures are established for transferring power to the vice president in case of presidential disability.

1968

Richard M. Nixon (Republican) is elected president, and Spiro Agnew (Republican) is elected vice president.

1972

President Richard M. Nixon and Vice President Spiro Agnew are reelected.

1973

The last remaining American combat troops are withdrawn from Vietnam in March.

Vice President Spiro Agnew resigns in October after pleading guilty to tax evasion. Gerald R. Ford (Republican) becomes vice president in December through the selection process outlined in the Twenty-Fifth Amendment.

1974

President Richard M. Nixon resigns from office in August due to the Watergate scandal. Vice President Gerald R. Ford succeeds to the presidency. Nelson Rockefeller (Republican) becomes vice president through the selection process outlined in the Twenty-Fifth Amendment. In September, Ford pardons Nixon for any crimes he may have committed related to Watergate.

1975

The Vietnam War ends in April with the fall of Saigon to the North Vietnamese communist government.

President Gerald R. Ford survives two assassination attempts in September, both in California and both by women assailants.

1976

Jimmy Carter (Democratic) is elected president, and Walter Mondale (Democratic) is elected vice president.

1980

Ronald Reagan (Republican) is elected president, and George H. W. Bush (Republican) is elected vice president.

1981

President Ronald Reagan survives an assassination attempt in March by John Hinckley Jr. in Washington, D.C.

1984

President Ronald Reagan and Vice President George H. W. Bush are reelected.

1988

George H. W. Bush (Republican) is elected president, and Dan Quayle (Republican) is elected vice president.

1992

Bill Clinton (Democratic) is elected president, and Al Gore (Democratic) is elected vice president.

1996

President Bill Clinton and Vice President Al Gore are reelected.

1998

President Bill Clinton is impeached by the House of Representatives but acquitted by the U.S. Senate on charges of lying under oath and obstruction of justice.

2000

George W. Bush (Republican) is elected president, and Richard Cheney (Republican) is elected vice president.

The U.S. Supreme Court rules in *Bush v. Gore* in December that the recount of votes within the state of Florida is unconstitutional, thereby awarding the state's Electoral College votes to George W. Bush to give him the victory in the presidential election over Democratic nominee Al Gore.

2004

President George W. Bush and Vice President Richard Cheney are reelected.

2008

Barack Obama (Democratic) is elected president, and Joseph Biden (Democratic) is elected vice president.

2012

President Barack Obama and Vice President Joseph Biden are reelected.

2016

Donald J. Trump (Republican) is elected president, and Mike Pence (Republican) is elected vice president.

2019

President Donald J. Trump is impeached by the House of Representatives in December but acquitted by the U.S. Senate in early 2020 on charges of abuse of power and obstruction of Congress.

2020

Joseph Biden (Democrat) is elected president, and Kamala Harris (Democrat) is elected vice president.

2021

President Donald J. Trump is impeached by the House of Representatives in January but acquitted by the U.S. Senate in February on one charge of incitement of insurrection related to the riots on January 6 at the U.S. Capitol.

1

Presidential Powers

"A government of laws, not of men" is a statement that is attributed to John Adams, the nation's second president (1797–1801). Adams codified the idea nearly two decades before becoming the president, as one of the architects of the 1780 Massachusetts state constitution. It is a phrase that is often used to describe the American system of government, as moving beyond the hold of a monarch was a seminal goal of the founding generation. For the framers of the U.S. Constitution, fear of political tyranny led to the design of a system of government based on separation of powers and checks and balances. The framers believed that individual liberty could not exist if legislative and executive powers were united in the same person or political institution. With this in mind, they established three branches of government separating the legislative, executive, and judicial responsibilities, as well as various checks and balances among the three branches.

Nearly every aspect of the nation's founding represented the founding fathers' fear of concentrated power in the hands of a few, and this is certainly evident in the design of the presidency. As James Madison wrote in *Federalist* 51, "If men were angels, no government would be necessary." The framers expected Congress, as the most representative of both the people and states, to be the dominant branch. As Madison also wrote in *Federalist* 51, "In republican government, the legislative authority necessarily predominates." The goal of the framers was to create "a more perfect union," a republic based on consent of the governed. However, ambivalence over the office of the president at the constitutional convention became a permanent feature of the American political system, as American citizens still confront the trade-off between tyranny and effectiveness when it comes to the chief executive.

Three models of the presidency that have emerged, based on the views of three of the most prominent members of the founding generation, provide an overview about the scope of presidential authority and expectations of how presidents govern. The first is the Madisonian Model, attributed to James Madison, who also served as America's fourth president (1809–1817). Prior to that, he was a coauthor of the *Federalist Papers* and is often referred to as the "Father of the Constitution." In this view, the president relies on Congress to lead in setting policies and mainly administers policies set by Congress.

Next is the Hamiltonian Model, named after Alexander Hamilton, also a coauthor of the *Federalist Papers* and the first treasury secretary during George Washington's administration. In *Federalist* 70, Hamilton advocated for an "energetic" executive: "A feeble executive implies a feeble execution of the government. A feeble execution is but another phrase for a bad execution: And a government ill executed, whatever it may be in theory, must be in practice a bad government." To Hamilton, the president should be heroic, rise above partisanship, and rely on the Constitution and public opinion for support. In Hamilton's view, the president should lead in all areas and ignore Congress if necessary.

Finally, Thomas Jefferson, the nation's third president (1801–1809) and author of the Declaration of Independence, provides another contrasting view of presidential power. Jefferson believed in a smaller, central government, and the Jeffersonian Model advocates for the president to lead through his party, acting similar to the role of a prime minister in a parliamentary system. The party, influenced and led by the president, sets the policy; the president then assists the party in getting its platform of goals and policies enacted.

Looking to the original intent of the framers does not provide a unified view of how the office of the presidency should be designed, nor does it give a blueprint for how presidents should behave while in office. While the Constitution does provide enumerated powers for the executive, the Constitution's silence on specifics has allowed presidents to expand their powers through implied and, or inherent powers. As this chapter will show, various presidents at different times in our nation's history have relied on a variety of interpretations of presidential powers to respond to crises and other challenges, political or otherwise.

First, a brief overview of the issues debated regarding the presidency at the Constitutional Convention shows that conflict and disagreement over the powers of the office have existed from the start. Next, we consider several theories of presidential power to help explain how the presidency has evolved since the early days of the republic. Finally, we look at several decisions by the U.S. Supreme Court that have defined presidential powers, particularly in the area of war powers, as the president's role as commander in chief has been an ongoing source of controversy for decades.

DEBATES AT THE CONSTITUTIONAL CONVENTION

One of the main issues discussed by those in attendance involved whether a single or plural executive should be created. The framers feared that a single leader would turn the new country into a monarchy. However, the main argument in *Federalist* 70 is Hamilton's argument for strong presidential leadership. The record is a bit unclear as to how much power the framers intended the president to have, yet the framers seemed willing to give the president broad powers as he was not to be popularly elected and would be constantly checked by Congress. It was also assumed that George Washington would serve as the first president and that he would help create important precedents and standards for the office and its role within the new government.

The length of a president's term and the method for presidential selection were also important considerations. The framers feared the creation of too much power if terms in office were made too long. The compromises became a four-year term (other possibilities discussed were terms as short as three years and as long as seven years) and the creation of the Electoral College (a more detailed discussion of this is provided in chapter 2) to avoid an election based on the popular vote. In addition, three requirements were created for eligibility: each president must be a natural-born citizen, must be at least 35 years of age, and have at least 14 years of residency in the United States.

Washington, elected with the unanimous support of the Electoral College in 1789, set an important precedent when he left office after two four-year terms in 1797. No president broke that precedent until Franklin D. Roosevelt sought and secured a third term in 1940 and was elected to a fourth term in 1944 (though he died just three months into the term in April 1945). Not long after, the Twenty-Second Amendment was ratified in 1951, which limited the president to two terms.

The issue of presidential succession has also been viewed by some as ambiguous. The problem first arose in 1841, when William Henry Harrison died after only a month in office. While the Constitution states that the vice president shall succeed to the office if the president cannot continue, the immediate question was whether Vice President John Tyler would assume the full duties and powers of the office or whether he would be viewed as an acting president until the next election. However, Tyler did assume the full duties and powers of the office, as did the eight other vice presidents who have succeeded to the office of the presidency.

Congress has also addressed presidential succession with several laws, the first of which was passed in 1792. The current presidential succession law, enacted in 1947, states that following the vice president, the next in line is the speaker of the House of Representatives, followed by the president pro tempore of the U.S. Senate, the secretary of State, the secretary of the Treasury, and each of the remaining cabinet officials based on the year the department was created (the secretary of Homeland Security is the 18th in line for the presidency, as the agency, which was created in 2002, is the newest among the cabinet positions).

The Constitution did not provide a remedy for a vice presidential vacancy, nor did it address the issue of presidential disability. Each time that a vice president succeeded to the presidency, the vice presidency remained vacant. An example of a president's inability to fulfill his duties was when Woodrow Wilson had a stroke during his second term in 1919, but the nation was unaware of the extent of his incapacitation. His wife, Edith, took on much of the responsibility of the office, allowing only a handful of White House officials access to her husband.

After John F. Kennedy's assassination in 1963, however, both issues were addressed through the Twenty-Fifth Amendment that was ratified in 1965. This amendment established a procedure for dealing with presidential disability, as well as the selection of a vice president. In addition, it clarified that the vice president becomes president (as opposed to acting president) upon death, resignation, or removal from office of the president.

According to Article I of the Constitution, a president can be impeached and removed from office for bribery, treason, and high crimes and misdemeanors. The House of Representatives has the authority to "impeach," which means to indict or bring charges against the president (or the vice president or all "civil officers" at the federal level, which includes legislators, cabinet members, and judges). Articles of impeachment can be approved with a simple majority vote in the House. The articles are then sent to the Senate for a trial, with senators serving as the jury and the Chief Justice of the United States presiding as judge (unless he or she is the one who has been impeached, in which case the most senior associate justice would preside instead). For conviction and removal, a two-thirds vote is required. High crimes and misdemeanors do not have a specific definition. A common law tradition exists that suggests that any personal misconduct is an impeachable offense; an impeachable offense does not have to be a criminal activity. Gerald Ford, while serving as Republican minority leader in the House during the 1960s, is known for saying that an impeachable offense is simply what a majority vote in the House deems it to be.

Three presidents have been impeached, but all three were acquitted during their Senate trials. Andrew Johnson was impeached in 1868, but the Senate failed by one vote for the required two-thirds majority on most of the articles to remove him from office. Most of the articles of impeachment brought against Johnson concerned his failure to implement congressional acts dealing with Reconstruction, as well as the tenure of office situation for many of Abraham Lincoln's cabinet members (Johnson succeeded to the presidency upon Lincoln's assassination in 1865, and Congress passed the Tenure of Office Act in 1867 in an attempt to stop Johnson from removing any executive officer or cabinet member who had been approved by the Senate). Bill Clinton was impeached in 1998, but both articles (one for lying under oath and the other for obstruction of justice) failed in the Senate in early 1999. Donald J. Trump was impeached in 2019 (for abuse of power and for obstruction of Congress) and again in 2021 (for incitement of insurrection), but the Senate failed to convict during both trials.

PRESIDENTIAL POWERS

Article II, Section 1, of the Constitution, stipulates that "executive power shall be vested" in the president of the United States, but unlike Article I, Section 8, which lists the enumerated powers of Congress, Article II, Section 1, lacks specificity in defining the presidency. As a result, the purpose, meaning, and relevance of the "vesting" clause have long been open to interpretation by presidents and scholars alike.

War Powers

Perhaps the most notable power that is listed in Article II, Section 1, is the president's role as commander in chief of the military. Specific yet mostly undefined, this presidential power has been one of the most debated elements of the Constitution in recent decades. The Constitution specifically grants Congress the power to declare war in Article I, Section 8, but of the more than 10 military conflicts in which the United States has participated since 1945, not one was sanctioned by a congressional declaration of war. In other words, while the United States has fought many wars since the end of World War II, the last time Congress invoked its constitutional authority to declare war was in 1941. All subsequent wars have been started by America's presidents. As members of Congress became more concerned with reelection than making tough decisions over which they could lose votes, they willingly relinquished the legislature's power to declare war. America's commanders in chief, on their part, gladly seized a power not granted to them by the Constitution, thereby enhancing their ability to pursue foreign-policy objectives without political impediments.

The controversy over the president's war powers escalated with congressional passage of the War Powers Resolution in 1973. Passed over Richard Nixon's veto, it requires America's commanders in chief to consult with Congress prior to the introduction of troops into any military theater, but it simultaneously recognizes a presidential power to respond to exigent circumstances without notification when such a notification would compromise the integrity or effectiveness of military action. The net effect of this concession was an acknowledgment in all but word of a presidential power to declare war through a statutory loophole that critics assert is clearly unconstitutional as it takes the authority to declare war away from Congress. Over the next four decades, every president beginning with Jimmy Carter (1977–1981) through Donald J. Trump (2017–present) has used this loophole to begin or augment American military operations all over the globe and secure a presidential power to declare war.

Law Enforcement

Article II, Section 3, of the Constitution, instructs the president to "take care that the laws [of the United States] be faithfully executed," which gives the president law-enforcement authority. While initially considered a limited authority, the executive branch has acquired extensive law-enforcement capabilities over the last century, and it wields considerable influence over agencies such as the Federal Bureau of Investigation, Drug Enforcement Administration, U.S. Secret Service, and several others that dominate national law-enforcement efforts. The leaders of these agencies, for example, serve at the pleasure of the president, who has the authority to replace them at any time.

The president's clemency power is also a crucial aspect of his executive authority. Clemency includes presidential pardons or the commutation of a sentence for crimes committed against the U.S. government. It has occasionally been used as the framers had intended—as a tool to achieve national reconciliation after turbulent political events, as exemplified by Gerald Ford's pardon of Richard Nixon following the Watergate scandal and Jimmy Carter's decision to grant amnesty to Vietnam-era draft evaders. In addition, recent presidents have also relied on the power to advance specific policies related to criminal justice reform. George W. Bush granted several pardons for those who had received mandatory sentencing (such as "three strikes" policies that became popular in an effort to combat the rise of crime in the 1990s), and Barack Obama's administration sought to shorten federal prison terms for nonviolent drug offenses. On December

19, 2016, Obama broke the record for the largest single-day use of the clemency power, granting 153 commutations and 78 pardons. In total, Obama granted clemency to 1,927 individuals (1,715 commutations and 212 pardons), surpassing all presidents but three: Franklin D. Roosevelt (3,687), Woodrow Wilson (2,480), and Harry Truman (2,044).

Critics assert, however, that the pardon power has become a political tool that presidential administrations sometimes use—often but not always in their waning days in power—to either reward key individuals and their political supporters for personal loyalty, financial contributions, and simple partisanship or indemnify themselves from potentially damaging legal and political scrutiny regarding specific presidential acts. Eleventh-hour pardons have become a standard of sorts, as presidents, aware that accountability and even popularity are largely irrelevant concerns during the dying hours of an outgoing administration, hurriedly issue dozens of reprieves, commutations, and other orders for executive clemency immediately prior to leaving office. Bill Clinton's pardon of fugitive financier Marc Rich may have been one of the more visible instances of political remuneration through executive clemency.

Legislative Authority

The framers strictly limited the president's constitutional role as head of government, giving the chief executive limited legislative authority. Presidents can approve legislation by signing a bill into law or veto (reject) a bill—though Congress can override the veto with a two-thirds majority vote in each house. Presidents can also present legislative priorities through the State of the Union message, the recommendation of potential legislation, and, in certain circumstances, the adjournment of Congress. The framers of the Constitution did not grant American presidents an active role in anything but the final stage of the legislative process, as they expected the president to devote most of his attention to issues related to national security, diplomacy, some economic policy, and law enforcement. Yet, Article II, Section 3, of the Constitution, suggests that the president is also a policymaker, if not the policymaker-in-chief. His responsibility to keep Congress apprised of administration objectives and to evaluate the nation's political course through the State of the Union message and his authority to present necessary legislation to Congress all reveal his inherent role as policymaker.

Appointment and Removal Power

The president's power to appoint judges, executive officials, and military officers has long been one of the most important tools for shaping the long-term political landscape. This is especially true regarding federal judges, as the president can choose who to nominate when any vacancy occurs. The nomination must be confirmed by a simple majority vote in the Senate, but once confirmed, the president's selection serves a lifetime term. The removal power is another matter. Federal judges serve based on good behavior, so their removal by the president, or others, for unimpeachable factors such as policy differences or ideological incompatibilities was a nonissue. However, that still left a sizable number of executive appointees who would serve at the pleasure of the party or parties to whom they were ultimately accountable. Who would have the authority to dismiss them? In most cases, presidents do, though this is not an absolute right. As the Supreme Court ruled in *Myers v. United States* (1926), presidents have the power to dismiss executive personnel as a logical element of presidential appointment authority and a necessary part of the constitutional duty to execute the laws of the United States.

Executive Privilege and Immunity

The Constitution does not explicitly refer to executive privilege or immunity in Article II or elsewhere. However, Article I, Section 6, of the Constitution, does identify specific immunities granted to members of Congress to protect them in the fulfillment of their legislative duties. Some observers and experts believe that this article implies that the president should be granted similar protections within the framework of separation of powers. An expert on the topic, political scientist Mark Rozell defines executive privilege as: "the right of the president and high-level executive branch officers to withhold information from Congress, the courts and ultimately the public" when it comes to "(1) certain national security needs and (2) protecting the privacy of White House deliberations when it is in the public interest to do so." In theory, executive privilege and immunity encourages candid conversations among the president and other executive branch officers when deliberating policy and doing the people's business.

Over the years, however—and especially since the 1970s—the Supreme Court has issued rulings that have denied the existence of an absolute immunity for the president. Most notably, the Supreme Court ruled in *U.S. v. Nixon* (1974) that executive privilege does exist, but that no one, not even the president, is completely above the law. The Court thus held that the president cannot use executive privilege as an excuse to withhold evidence that is "demonstrably relevant in a criminal trial." The Supreme Court also recognized broad presidential immunity against civil suits involving claims stemming from their official actions in *Nixon v. Fitzgerald* (1982). But in *Clinton v. Jones* (1997), the Supreme Court held that presidential immunity does not extend to suits involving the president's private conduct, and it allowed a sexual harassment lawsuit brought against Clinton by former Arkansas state employee Paula Jones to go forward prior to the end of Clinton's term.

EXPANSION OF PRESIDENTIAL POWERS

History has shown an expansion of presidential powers beyond what the framers originally intended for the office. Generally, presidents themselves have expanded the powers of their office during times of crises by adopting broad interpretations of their responsibilities thanks to "the silences of the Constitution." However, presidents have also viewed their own powers in office differently, depending on the state of the economy and world affairs. Presidential personalities can also determine much about how presidential power is exercised. For example, Franklin D. Roosevelt faced a severe economic crisis when he first took office in 1933 and exercised many presidential powers to combat the Great Depression, yet his actions remain controversial as some argue they were extra-constitutional (those that stretched the assumed powers of the office) or even unconstitutional.

The first several men to hold the office of the presidency set important early precedents regarding presidential powers. The framers believed that not only would Washington be the first president but that he would shape the office in important ways for future occupants. Washington set several important precedents, such as only serving two terms. He also set the precedent that department heads should support the president's policies, going beyond the Constitution's suggestion to receive written opinions on policy matters. Washington also believed that presidents, not Congress, should determine which foreign ambassadors to receive or which foreign countries should be granted diplomatic recognition. Thomas Jefferson also played an important role in the early development of presidential powers. Jefferson often responded to political, rather than legal, considerations, such as the Louisiana Purchase in 1803, considered controversial because the Constitution did not grant specific powers to the president to acquire new territory. Jefferson was also the first president to govern through leadership of (what would now be considered) a political party, and he dominated the affairs of Congress through his leadership of Democratic-Republicans (a group of congressional members opposed to Federalist policies that allied together prior to the creation of what are now considered to be political parties). As a result, Jefferson never had to veto legislation, because no bill that he seriously opposed ever reached his desk for consideration.

Since that time, the actions of subsequent presidents have led to the development of numerous theories to explain the constitutional role of presidential power. For example, the prerogative theory of the presidency is most often attributed to Abraham Lincoln, who stretched the emergency powers of the office more than any other president due to the Civil War. Lincoln unilaterally authorized many decisions and then called Congress back into session to make them legitimate; he called up the militia and volunteers, blockaded southern ports, expanded the army and navy beyond statute limitations, closed the mails to treasonous correspondence, arrested persons suspected of disloyalty, and suspended the writ of habeas corpus. Lincoln justified his actions by pointing to both his powers as commander in chief and the "vesting" and "take care" clauses of the Constitution: "I have never understood that the presidency conferred upon me an unrestricted right to act. . . . I did understand, however, that my oath to preserve the Constitution to the best of my ability imposed upon me the duty of preserving, by every indispensable means, that government—that nation, of which the Constitution was the organic law."

Theodore Roosevelt advocated the stewardship doctrine, which supports expanding the role and powers of the president, as long as it is done in the public interest and does not directly violate the Constitution. At the turn of the twentieth century, Roosevelt ushered in what is often referred to as the rhetorical presidency. Regarding himself as the steward of the people, he effectively used what he called the "bully pulpit"—the stature of the White House—to speak out loudly and persistently to the American public on the issues and affairs of the day. Like Lincoln, he found broad powers within the vesting and take care clauses and saw the president as an agent of social and economic reform. He called his domestic program the "Square Deal," which focused on three main issues: conservation of natural resources, control of corporations, and consumer protection. Roosevelt also greatly enhanced the role of the president as a statesman in the international arena, initiating the building of the Panama Canal, expanding the size and scope of the U.S. Navy, and intervening militarily in several nations (most notably in Latin America). The latter, which began to move the United States away from its traditional isolationist posture, is known as "Roosevelt's Corollary" to the Monroe Doctrine. The Monroe Doctrine, first introduced in 1823 by James Monroe, stated that the United States would view further efforts by European countries to colonize land in the Americas as an act of aggression.

William Howard Taft, Roosevelt's immediate successor, reversed course regarding presidential powers through his literalist approach. Also known as the Whig theory, Taft's literalist approach reflected a belief that the president should only have those powers as specifically outlined in the Constitution. Taft's deference to Congress, as well as his move away from the public connection with the Oval Office that Roosevelt had developed, contributed to Taft's failure to win reelection in 1912. Of course,

Roosevelt's entrance in that year's presidential election as a third-party candidate, challenging his former friend and political ally, also helped to open the door to Woodrow Wilson's election that November.

Wilson, a political scientist, former president of Princeton University, and former governor of New Jersey, believed in strong presidential powers. Wilson sought to exercise fully the powers of the office (particularly through his unitary approach in leading the nation into World War I). Whereas Theodore Roosevelt had sought to link the presidency directly to the people by reducing the influence of political parties, Wilson instead wanted to make the president a strong party leader. His view of the Constitution, according to presidential scholar Saladin M. Ambar, "was based on a notion that government is made to adapt to changing times—with the chief executive leading the way—as opposed to the more restrained notion of governmental power so esteemed by the founders."

Lincoln, Roosevelt, and Wilson led the charge toward a more modern presidency capable of accommodating greater authority and expanded resources. During the late 1940s and into the early 1950s, presidential power continued to expand as the American economy grew in global importance and the United States committed itself to combatting the spread of communism during the Cold War. By the late 1960s and early 1970s, the presidencies of Lyndon Johnson and Richard Nixon had been labeled as "imperial," due mostly to the actions of each regarding the use of military force in Vietnam (and in Nixon's case, surrounding Southeast Asian countries as well) in an attempt to stop the spread of communism.

JUDICIAL CHECKS ON PRESIDENTIAL POWERS

Just as the president and Congress expanded their authority over social and economic issues during the Great Depression in the 1930s, so too did presidents expand their powers to address the military and diplomatic crises unleashed by the Cold War following World War II. The consequence has been what some would argue to be an unconstitutional expansion of federal governmental authority in ways that would have been unthinkable to the framers.

In general, the Supreme Court has been willing to allow expansion of executive power over constitutional objections. Two cases, however, illustrated the Court's willingness to define the issue of inherent powers when dealing with domestic issues. In *Youngstown Sheet & Tube Company v. Sawyer* (1952), the Court struck down Harry Truman's seizure of the nation's steel mills, rejecting Truman's argument that he had inherent executive power to take that action to protect the domestic economy and bolster the Korean War effort. The Court recognized an inherent executive power in Article II, but nevertheless, it found Truman's action to be impermissible as Congress had already considered and rejected legislation permitting such an executive order in response to a strike, which is what occurred within the steel industry. This case was a reminder that expansion of presidential power is not without limitation and that the president's actions within the domestic sphere are subject to judicial scrutiny. Similarly, in 1971 President Richard Nixon sent his Attorney General John Mitchell into federal district court to seek an injunction against the *New York Times* for its series of stories on the Pentagon Papers, leaked classified documents (a 47-volume study) detailing the history of United States' involvement in Vietnam. In *New York Times Company v. United States* (1971), however, the Court declared that publication of the Pentagon Papers was not a national security threat, clearing the way for the newspaper to continue publishing excerpts. The ruling was a victory for advocates of freedom of the press and a rebuke to Nixon.

Regarding foreign policy, as early as 1936, the Supreme Court gave its approval on presidential primacy in *United States v. Curtiss-Wright Export Corporation*. In 1934, Congress had adopted a joint resolution authorizing the president to prohibit U.S. companies from selling munitions to the warring nations of Paraguay and Bolivia. Congress also provided for criminal penalties for those violating presidential prohibitions. Curtiss-Wright brought suit, claiming that Congress had unconstitutionally delegated its lawmaking powers to the president. Despite the Court having ruled against delegation of legislative power in domestic issues in *Schechter Poultry Corporation v. United States* (1935) a year earlier, the Court said that the delegation of power was constitutional when dealing with foreign affairs. The Court referred to the president as the "sole organ of the federal government in the field of international relations." This decision was based on the belief, first articulated by John Marshall when he was a member of the House of Representatives in 1799 (Marshall would become Chief Justice of the United States in 1801), that presidents should have independence when acting with regard to foreign policy. This is similar to unitary executive theory, which holds that the president controls the entire executive branch based on the vesting clause in Article II.

Since that time, the Court has often confirmed the president's broad powers in the foreign policy arena. Presidents have authority to make treaties with foreign nations with the advice and consent of the Senate. The broad scope of this power was endorsed by the Supreme Court in *Missouri v. Holland* (1920), which involved a treaty between the United States and Great Britain involving migratory birds from Canada. The Court rejected the claim made by Missouri that Congress did not have the authority to pass regulations contained in that treaty against the killing of such birds. Presidents also use executive agreements as an alternative to treaties or use them to implement treaty provisions. Unlike treaties, executive agreements do not require approval by the Senate. Valid executive agreements are legally equivalent to treaties, but presidents often use them to bypass Congress. Most involve minor matters of international concern, such as specification of the details of postal relations or the use of radio airwaves. The president can also terminate a treaty without Senate approval, as determined by the Court in *Goldwater v. Carter* (1979), which dealt with the termination of a defense treaty with Taiwan.

Presidential power to act in a national emergency and to commit military forces to combat situations has a long heritage. The president is the commander in chief, yet Congress has the power to declare war. The commander in chief may need to "repel sudden attacks" but must share power in this regard with the Congress to protect against the possible abuse of presidential power in waging war. In *Ex parte Merryman* (1861), Chief Justice Roger Taney declared Lincoln's suspension of habeas corpus during the Civil War to be unconstitutional on the grounds that only Congress has the power to suspend the writ "when in Cases of Rebellion or Invasion the public Safety may require it." In *The Prize Cases* (1863), the Court acknowledged the necessity of deferring to the president's decisions in times of crisis. With the absence of a formal declaration of war from the Congress, Lincoln in 1863 ordered the capture of vessels by the Union navy during the blockade of Southern ports. Under the existing law at the time, the vessels would become the property of the Union only with a formal declaration of war. But the Court found the seizures to be legal, stating that "the President is not only authorized, but bound to resist force. He does not initiate the war, but is bound to accept the challenge without waiting for any special legislative authority."

Another difficult constitutional question involves the extent of presidential power in the domestic sphere during wartime, especially as it relates to the rights of American citizens. The Court has given mixed answers to this question. For example, in *Ex Parte Milligan* (1866), the Court declared that Lincoln's orders for the trial of civilians by military courts were unconstitutional. Yet, in one of its more infamous rulings in *Korematsu v. U.S.* (1944), the Court declared constitutional the internment of Japanese Americans by the Franklin D. Roosevelt administration during World War II (in 1988, Ronald Reagan signed a legislation providing reparations to those same Japanese-American families).

These types of issues would again come before the Supreme Court following the September 11, 2001, terrorist attacks against the United States and the subsequent applications of presidential authority by the George W. Bush administration. The Bush administration argued that as a war-time president, Bush had greatly expanded constitutional authorities to combat terrorism and protect national security. He and his advisors relied on the unitary executive theory regarding many of their actions in the weeks and months following 9/11. For example, Bush claimed that he had the authority to indefinitely detain foreign nationals as well as U.S. citizens determined to be "enemy combatants" at Guantanamo Bay. However, the Supreme Court did not always concur with Bush's interpretation of presidential powers. In *Rasul v. Bush* (2004), the Court rejected the claim that federal courts lacked jurisdiction over foreign nationals held in Cuba and affirmed the right of these individuals to seek judicial review of the basis for their detention. In *Hamdi v. Rumsfeld* (2004), the Court ruled that the president has a right to detain U.S. citizens as enemy combatants but that citizens have a right to consult with an attorney and to contest the basis for their detention before an independent tribunal. The right to hold an enemy combatant indefinitely was not granted under the Authorization for Use of Military Force passed by Congress to fight terrorism after 9/11. In *Hamdan v. Rumsfeld* (2006), the Court ruled that military commissions set up by the Bush administration lack "the power to proceed because its structures and procedures violate both the Uniform Code of Military Justice and the four Geneva Conventions signed in 1949." And in *Boumediene v. Bush* (2008), the Court ruled that foreign terrorist suspects held at Guantanamo Bay have constitutional rights to challenge their detention in U.S. courts.

CONCLUSION

While the office of the president and its associated powers may look nothing like what the framers intended, the irony is that the office has only been changed nominally through amendments that address the presidency. The powers of the office have expanded due to the fact that some presidents took bold action in the face of economic or military crises in what they considered the interests of the people and the nation. A never-ending debate has ensued as a result—have presidents acted beyond the scope of their constitutional powers, or do the "silences" in the Constitution give presidents authority to govern as they see fit? The Constitution is at times contradictory. For example, although serving as commander in chief is an enumerated power under the Constitution, the vague description of that power in the document has allowed numerous presidents to wage war through inherent or implied powers without congressional approval. In addition, while presidents have few unilateral powers, they do have a range of authority over executive branch agencies (which we will discuss further in chapter 6). Presidents also remain at the mercy of legislative and judicial checks on their power, though at many points in the nation's history, both Congress and the Supreme Court have sanctioned expansions of presidential power (though not always). Regardless of one's view of appropriate presidential authority within the Constitution, it is important to note that significant social and economic changes have occurred since World War II, along with ever-changing national security and defense issues, and that presidents must react swiftly to changing world events. As a result, the individuals who have held the office of the presidency have played just as important a role in shaping presidential powers as have the changes to the institution itself.

2

Presidential Elections

Electing a president is a long and, at times, complicated endeavor. The process that has emerged since the mid-twentieth century looks vastly different from what the framers had in mind when they designed the Electoral College. In fact, the Electoral College was crafted for the specific purpose of keeping presidential selection out of the hands of the mass public. Today the Electoral College is still the final step in electing a president, but ordinary American citizens are much more central to the voting process. To garner support from these citizens, numerous strategies are employed by candidates regarding media, money, and public opinion. These are all designed to attract voter support in each of the three phases of a presidential campaign—the pre-nomination phase, the nomination phase (which includes all primary and caucus contests as well as the nominating conventions), and the general election. In this chapter, we look at both process and strategies of contemporary presidential campaigns—and how positions taken and promises made on the campaign trail can complicate transitions from campaign mode to governing.

THE PRE-NOMINATION PHASE

It seems that presidential campaigns in the United States never end. No sooner has a winner been declared on Election Night (with the exception of the closely contested and controversial George W. Bush versus Al Gore race in 2000, which ended only after a ruling from the U.S. Supreme Court 35 days after election night) than the news media is already predicting potential winners and losers for the next campaign. In fact, news media speculation about the contest that is four years away often begins a few weeks prior to the conclusion of the current campaign, especially if one candidate has maintained a solid lead (as Barack Obama did in 2008), or the news media is convinced they know who will win (as in 2016, when most news organizations incorrectly believed that Hillary Clinton would be victorious). The high cost of a presidential campaign also requires that potential candidates start planning their fundraising efforts early. During the 2016 presidential campaign cycle, $1.5 billion was raised by all candidates. President Donald Trump declared his reelection bid on the day he took office in 2017, and by early 2020, he had raised roughly $160 million. In addition, the intricacy with which voters are now microtargeted during both the primary and general election campaign, the emphasis on get-out-the-vote efforts, and the challenge of putting together a team of campaign advisors, strategists, and pollsters make the entire process of running for president a massive undertaking. The bottom line is that the sooner candidates start running, even before officially declaring their candidacy, the better their chance of succeeding.

First dubbed the "invisible primary" by journalist Arthur Hadley in 1976, the pre-nomination period is the time span between the end of a presidential election and the first primary of the next election. During this period, presidential candidates are vetted by news media, party leaders, and interest groups, and one candidate often emerges as the early front-runner to secure the party's nomination. Two things seem to matter more than anything else during the invisible primary—money and media exposure. This has become particularly true in recent years with the front-loading of primaries (which means that more primary contests are held earlier in the calendar year). During the long preprimary phase, candidates must raise large sums of money, hire campaign staffs, shape their messages on numerous issues, gain visibility among party elites to obtain high-profile endorsements, and vie to be taken seriously by the news media.

Most presidential candidates do not decide to seek the White House on a whim. Numerous factors go into making the decision to run, including the heavy emotional and physical toll that running for president can take on both the candidate and his or her family. The act of campaigning can begin months, or even years, before a candidate faces any voters in a state nominating contest. The constitutional requirements for the job of president are minimal—candidates only need to be 35 years of age, a natural born citizen, and residents of the United States for at least 14 years—but the unofficial requirements can include prior political experience, name recognition, party support, adequate financial resources, strong appeal to the party's base during the primaries, strong appeal to independent voters during the general election, and strong leadership and communication skills. Self-confidence, obviously, is a must; a presidential candidate must believe that not only can he or she handle the campaign, but that if elected, he or she can succeed as president and commander in chief.

Once a candidate either files the paperwork with the FEC to create an exploratory committee or officially announces his or her candidacy, fund-raising becomes a top priority. Raising money throughout the entire campaign is important, but early money is crucial, as perhaps nothing else signals as strongly to the political world that a candidate is indeed viable and competitive. Early money can buy name recognition and favorable coverage for those who need it, particularly for candidates without a national reputation at the start of the race. Raising large sums of money will certainly get the attention of the news media and can also discourage potential rivals from joining the race. The news media is key in determining a candidate's viability, and the strength of fundraising is one of the factors that goes into that equation. In addition to media attention and name recognition, early money can also allow a candidate to hire talented and experienced campaign staff and create an effective field organization in early primary and caucus states.

In addition to successful fundraising, the news media also consider candidates to be viable based on the hiring of well-known (at least within political circles) campaign strategists and advisors as well as results from early public opinion polling. Money, media, and polling contribute to what is called "momentum" during a presidential campaign. Momentum is particularly important during the early primary and caucuses, but it also plays a role throughout the invisible primary.

Not all candidates survive for more than a few months, particularly when a crowded field of contenders are all jockeying for "serious contender" status. In 2016, a total of 17 candidates ran for the Republican nomination, and in 2020, nearly 30 candidates sought the Democratic nomination. Both cases represent what are called "open" primaries, meaning that an incumbent president or vice president is not among those seeking the party nomination. Only a handful are placed in the top tier by news media coverage; the others never break through to the top tier and as a result do not receive much attention from voters or donors.

What is called horse-race coverage begins in the pre-nomination phase, which means that the news media report on a daily basis about who's ahead and who's behind in terms of fundraising and public opinion polls well before any votes are even cast. The media attention focused on this early aspect of the presidential campaign has, in recent years, made the invisible primary not-so-invisible, which has not only extended the length of the overall presidential campaign but also raised the bar for candidates. In this environment, an early campaign misstep or slow start can be fatal for a candidate's White House aspirations.

THE NOMINATION PHASE

Once voting begins during the nomination phase of a presidential campaign, candidates often have little to no room for error as political fortunes can change within days or even hours thanks to news media scrutiny. This is perhaps the most intense and tumultuous part of the campaign. The field of candidates is typically still crowded, media coverage is intense, and campaigns have to prepare to compete in 50-plus contests across the country (primaries and caucuses are held in all 50 states plus the District of Columbia, Puerto Rico, Guam, and other U.S. territories). Moreover, primaries and caucuses are spread out over several months and governed by different rules set by the state party organizations. The primary contests can be an unpredictable free-for-all in an attempt to woo voters and secure delegates to the national conventions.

A perfect candidate does not exist, as certain candidates and certain strategies will have an advantage over others during certain campaigns, meaning that the political environment can dictate much of the circumstances in elevating one candidate over others. Candidates must have an effective strategy for getting supporters to go to their local polling place and vote. A campaign's ability to turn out supportive voters on Election Day is sometimes known as its "ground game," and it typically depends on the ability to develop grassroots organizations at the state, district, and precinct levels and to recruit campaign volunteers.

Grassroots support is essential for candidates looking to generate momentum for their campaigns. Several factors contribute to momentum, including name recognition, support from national and state party officials, media attention, standing in public opinion polls, and fundraising. While momentum during the invisible primary is also important (think money raised or media recognition earned), once voters get involved, the results are even more tangible. A candidate either does well enough in the first handful of primary and caucus contests to keep going or has a poor showing and has to end his or her campaign. Various components of momentum work in tandem; for example, a win or second-place finish in Iowa or New Hampshire (always the first two presidential nominating contests) can generate positive media attention, which can then in turn spur higher standing in public opinion polls or increased contributions to the campaign. Similarly, an uptick in public opinion poll standing or an increase in financial contributions to a campaign can get the media's attention and generate positive coverage, which might get the attention of voters.

Understanding the importance of the early contests and how the primary calendar affects campaign strategy is crucial. The Iowa Caucuses are always the first nomination contest, followed by the New Hampshire Primary. Both contests occurred during the first week of January in 2008 and in 2012, and then early February in 2016 and 2020, even though they used to be held as late as April.

This calendar change is due to a process called front-loading. Since 1996, many states have moved their nominating contests earlier on the primary calendar in an effort to force candidates to give more attention to issues of special importance to voters in those states and to have a greater say in the nomination process. For example, California traditionally held its presidential primary on the first Tuesday of June. But, during most presidential campaigns, the nominee for each major party would have already been unofficially decided by capturing enough delegates to secure the party's nomination in earlier contests. The state thus moved up its primary by three months, to early March, for the 2020 election.

Proponents of front-loading are quick to point out the downside to allowing two small states such as Iowa and New Hampshire, both of which have a much higher percentage of white residents than the nation as a whole, to go first. These critics assert that those states should not play such a pivotal role in anointing front-runners for party nominations or winnowing down the presidential field. Yet, supporters of Iowa and New Hampshire keeping their status as the first nominating contests argue that the small size of each state allows for candidates to engage in "retail politics," meaning that presidential aspirants must campaign in a way that puts them in direct contact with voters in cities, towns, and counties throughout each state.

The nomination process for both Democrats and Republicans comes through winning a majority of delegates to the national party convention. While each party, and each state, can differ in how it awards delegates after a primary or caucus (some states do a winner-take-all system, while others allocate delegates based on proportional vote schemes), the candidate with a majority of the total delegates at the convention will become the party's nominee. Each party holds a nominating convention during the summer months to officially nominate their candidates for president and vice president and to adopt a party's official platform (a statement that includes a variety of policy positions that party members have approved).

GENERAL ELECTION

The final phase of the presidential campaign, the general election, begins after each party has officially nominated their candidates. Labor

Day weekend is often seen as the unofficial start of the final push to Election Day, but in reality, political commercials and campaign rallies for the general election often predate Labor Day. Once it becomes clear who the party nominee is going to be, that candidate and the party for which he or she is serving as standard bearer typically shifts his or her attention toward their general election foe.

Several factors come into play when developing campaign strategies, including the Electoral College, money, voter turnout, campaign communications, presidential debates, and running mates.

THE ELECTORAL COLLEGE

The Electoral College—not the national popular vote—determines the winner of each presidential election. All but two states rely on a winner-take-all system of awarding electoral votes, which means that if a candidate wins the popular vote in a state, then he or she wins all of that state's electoral votes. Only Maine and Nebraska do not rely on the winner-take-all system. Instead, the candidate who wins each congressional district in those states wins that electoral vote, while the candidate who wins the popular vote in the state wins the two votes represented by the state's two seats in the U.S. Senate. After Election Day, the Electors then vote in December at their state capital, and more than half the states have laws that require the Electors to vote for the party nominee that they have been chosen to represent. On very rare occasions, "faithless electors" have cast their vote for someone other than the candidate on their slate, though this has never affected the outcome of a presidential election. Serving as an Elector is considered a symbolic reward (often for party loyalty) more so than an opportunity to influence the election outcome.

Created by the framers to insulate the presidency from popular rule among the mass public, the Electoral College influences election strategy and imposes strategic decision-making on candidates based on the allocation of votes. A total of 538 Electoral College votes are available. This figure is based on the 435 seats in the House of Representatives, 100 seats in the Senate, and the three votes given to the District of Columbia by the Twenty-Third Amendment, which was ratified in 1964. A simple majority—270—is required to win the election. The most populous states have the most Electoral College votes, while the least populous states have the fewest. The three largest states in the nation have consistently voted for one party in recent decades—a Republican candidate has not won California since 1988 or New York since 1984 and a Democratic candidate has not won Texas since 1976. As a result, these states—and other states with a pronounced slant toward one party or the other—typically receive little attention from either campaign. Candidates will still travel to these states for fundraising events, but when it comes to targeting voters, campaigns focus most heavily on so-called swing states. These are states that are neither decisively "Blue" (a shorthand designation for Democrat-friendly states with higher percentages of liberal voters) nor clearly "Red" (Republican-leaning states with large numbers of conservative voters).

Swing states receive more attention than other states during the campaign in the form of campaign stops by the candidate and his or her surrogates, as well as voter registration and get-out-the-vote efforts. The news media also focus more heavily on these states since they often determine who will emerge victorious on Election Night. Voter participation in these states can also be higher than in noncompetitive states since so much attention is focused on voter mobilization efforts. The number of swing states in recent campaigns is often between 10 and 12, and the most prominent among them have included Florida, Ohio, Pennsylvania, Virginia, Michigan, Wisconsin, Colorado, and Nevada. In effect, the Electoral College discourages presidential candidates from running in all 50 states, since it makes no sense to waste campaign resources in lightly populated states with only a few electoral votes or in large states that are clearly going to vote for one candidate over the other.

A candidate can win the popular vote yet still lose the election by not securing the necessary 270 electoral votes. In 2016, for example, Republican nominee Donald Trump won the Electoral College, and thus the presidency, even though his opponent, Democrat Hillary Clinton, won the popular vote by roughly 3 million votes. Similarly, in 2000, Democratic nominee Al Gore beat Republican candidate George W. Bush in the number of total votes cast by roughly 500,000, but Bush won the Electoral College by 271–266 when the U.S. Supreme Court issued a decision (*Bush v. Gore*) that for all practical purposes awarded Florida's 25 electoral votes to Bush. Prior to that, the only other time when a popular-vote winner had lost the Electoral College—and thus the presidency—was in 1888, when Benjamin Harrison beat incumbent Grover Cleveland.

MONEY

Candidates in presidential elections rely on various sources of money to fund their campaigns, including individual donors, political parties, PACs, and Super PACs. Some candidates, such as Donald Trump in 2016, have also drawn from their own personal fortunes to help pay for their campaigns.

In the 1970s, Congress passed campaign finance reform legislation that was intended to decrease the influence of money in presidential campaigns.

Since then, however, other legislation and several momentous Supreme Court rulings have opened the floodgates for virtually unregulated campaign contributions of millions of dollars from corporations, unions, and other powerful political players. As a result, the idea of publicly funded campaigns (meant to level the playing field and reduce the influence of powerful monied interests in American politics) is mostly a thing of the past.

After Congress reformed the campaign finance system with passage of the Federal Election Campaign Act of 1974, the funding for each subsequent general election campaign came from the Presidential Election Campaign Fund (PECF) until Barack Obama's decision to forego public funding in 2008. The money in this fund comes from what is known as a tax checkoff, which allows tax payers to designate money for the PECF by checking a box on their federal income tax return instructing the Internal Revenue Service to earmark $3 from federal taxes already owed to be placed in the fund. During the general election, major party candidates then receive their public funding grant from the federal government. By accepting the funds, each candidate agrees to the same campaign spending limit. In 2004, George W. Bush and John Kerry each received just under $75 million to pay for their general election campaigns. In 2008, John McCain received $84.1 million in public funds to conduct his general election campaign (and under federal law, he was allowed to raise an additional $46.4 million for legal and accounting expenses). Obama, however, decided not to accept the federal funds as he had raised the record-breaking total of $745.7 million in private funds for his primary nomination and general election campaign. Obama's refusal marked the first time in the history of presidential public financing that a major party nominee had declined to accept the general election grant (and with it the attached spending limit). In 2012 and 2016, each of the major party nominees opted out of the available federal funding for the general election.

By the 1990s, a large part of presidential campaigns (with dollar amounts in the hundreds of millions) were being bankrolled by soft money contributions. These unlimited contributions were being raised by political parties and PACs for various expenditures (like voter education in the form of advertising or get-out-the-vote efforts), as opposed to hard money contributions made directly to candidates (and thus subject to federal contribution limits). In 2002, Congress passed the Bipartisan Campaign Reform Act, which in effect banned soft money contributions. In 2003, the U.S. Supreme Court ruled in *McConnell v. FEC* that the ban on soft money contributions was indeed constitutional. While many had hoped that banning soft money from presidential elections would bring down the overall costs, the ban served to create new and more innovative loopholes as campaign spending by presidential candidates hit all-time highs during the next three election cycles. In 2004, many big money donors who had been used to making large soft money contributions directly to the political parties instead began giving money to interest groups through tax-exempt organizations (called 527s because of the related IRS code that allows such groups to spend unlimited amounts of money as long as they do not "expressly advocate" for a particular candidate or coordinate their election activities with a particular campaign). By 2008, both Obama and his Republican rival, John McCain, made public pleas to their supporters to send contributions to their campaigns directly and not to 527 groups.

Then, in 2010, the Supreme Court issued another ruling regarding the regulation of money that changed the campaign finance landscape of presidential campaigns yet again. In *Citizens United vs. The Federal Election Commission*, the Court overturned previous restrictions on electioneering communications as well as the long-standing ban on corporations and labor unions contributing to political action committees (PACs). Easing the restrictions on corporations and labor unions paved the way for the emergence of so-called Super PACs, which could accept unlimited contributions from wealthy donors. The money raised and spent by each Super PAC had no limit, as long as there was no coordination between the Super PAC and a particular campaign. Since then, a majority of Super PAC money has been spent on negative attack ads.

VOTER TURNOUT AND PREFERENCE

Voter turnout—the ability of campaigns to motivate supporters of their candidate to actually vote for him or her—has long been recognized as a key factor in presidential elections. This is part of what is referred to as the "ground game," which includes a campaign's ability to register voters, promoting a candidate through door-to-door canvassing and talking to potential voters and even providing rides to polling locations for voters on Election Day. Voter preference is also an important part of this equation. Political socialization plays a large role in how potential voters perceive candidates, policy issues, and political parties. Influences such as family, peers, education, mass media, and various other demographic factors (such as socioeconomic status, gender, and religion) all work together to shape political and ideological values and beliefs. This, in turn, can determine an individual's affinity for a political party or candidate (or lack thereof), as well as that individual's level of motivation to vote in any given election. One of the main strategic considerations of a presidential campaign, then, is not only how to appeal to a wide variety of voters but also how to get those same voters to show up on Election Day.

Major studies by political scientists in the area of voting behavior have developed two basic models. One explains voting as a prospective behavior, meaning that voters consider the policy positions of the current candidates and their respective parties to make a choice. The other suggests that voters behave retrospectively, meaning that voters assess the performance of current officeholders in such areas as the economy or national security in deciding whether to support them with their vote. For incumbent presidents, the retrospective model generally is beneficial to their reelection prospects if, for example, the economy is strong or improving and the nation is at peace. Partisanship—identification with and allegiance to a political party—also plays an important role in voting behavior. Partisan cues help voters decide which candidate they will support or whether they will even vote. Certain policy issues or personal characteristics of a candidate can play a greater role for voters in a presidential election who do not have strong partisan feelings.

Partisanship was not always as evident in voting patterns as it is today. In the 1970s and 1980s, voters were more likely to engage in split-ticket voting (for example, voting for one party's presidential candidate while voting for another party's congressional candidate) than they are today. During those years, voters relied less on party identification and more on the characteristics of individual candidates when making a decision about whom to support. This trend of "candidate-centered" politics was a result of numerous factors, including social and economic changes, political upheaval from events such as the Vietnam War and Watergate, and a news media landscape that was not as fragmented or as partisan as it is today. Whereas most American voters of that era got their news from the same handful of generally moderate networks, national news magazines, and newspaper syndicates, large sectors of the American public today choose to get their news from conservative or liberal sources—a state of affairs that greatly limits their exposure to different ideas and viewpoints.

Reaching uncommitted, or less partisan, voters during a presidential campaign is thus of prime importance. Once a candidate has earned his or her party's nomination, they are in effect the party's standard bearer, so attention shifts during the general election to voter turnout as well as reaching independent voters in swing states. Since the 2008 and 2012 campaigns, technology has played an increasingly important role in get-out-the-vote efforts through what is known as "micro-targeting" of swing voters. Data is collected on voters in swing states to determine the level of support each person might have for a candidate and the likelihood they will vote. Voter files were developed with the following information: name, address, age, party affiliation, and voter participation in previous elections. Then census data showing ethnicity, income, and education was added, along with commercial data about consumer preferences, data about financial contributions, use of lawn signs, or responses to phone calls during past the campaigns. All this is done to develop a probability score about whether each voter is likely to support a candidate and to develop potential micro-targeted advertising.

CAMPAIGN COMMUNICATIONS

Voters now have a growing number of choices about how to obtain information about presidential candidates and their policy priorities. While voters used to rely on getting information during the presidential campaign from traditional news sources such as television, newspapers, and weekly newsmagazines, voters now can turn to many other new media sources. Indeed, the changes in media use during presidential campaigns have been dramatic. The first candidate webpages appeared in 1996, and online fundraising success got its start with John McCain's primary campaign in 2000 (he raised $1 million online after beating George W. Bush in the New Hampshire Republican primary, which at the time was considered a huge sum of money). Since then, as available technologies for the Internet and cell phones have rapidly expanded, so too has the presence of social media (Facebook, YouTube, Twitter, Instagram, etc.), numerous political blogs, and other sources of online news.

CAMPAIGN ADVERTISEMENTS

Television ads are still widely used in campaigns, though they do not have the same effect they once did as they are but one of many messaging techniques within today's saturated media environment. Some of the most effective and memorable campaign ads over the years have been positive in their message, but many are oriented toward trying to negatively define opponents in the minds of voters—often by distorting their records. Candidate webpages are still seen as a staple and a good way to communicate directly to voters in an unmediated fashion, but a presence on social media is also expected. Technology has not only allowed campaigns to develop more direct means of getting their message out to voters, but the information provided by voters on candidate webpages or through cell phone apps also provide data mining opportunities to the campaign to micro-target messaging to potential voters and supplement its fundraising efforts.

Media coverage of the general election campaign plays a large role in setting the tone of the campaign as well as shaping the overall political environment. For loyal partisan voters, media coverage is unlikely to affect voter choice, although it could influence their decision to participate. For independent voters, the content and quality of information from news sources can have a more prominent effect on decision-making. Media coverage also directly shapes campaign communication strategies. The preference for press coverage that focuses on the horse race of the campaign begins in the invisible primary and carries through to Election Day. Much of the coverage during the general election focuses on day-to-day tracking polls at the national level (which is not always relevant given that presidents are not elected by popular vote) or in swing states to determine the potential outcome in the Electoral College. The trend toward an emphasis on "soft news" (personal stories about the candidate, horse race coverage, internal squabbling or strategizing within a campaign, etc.) than "hard news" (news analysis of major policy issues and the candidate's stance on such issues) has also continued, to the dismay of many Americans and journalism critics. This sensationalistic coverage is particularly evident not only on television with cable news but also on network news and local news.

The pervasive coverage of polling during the general election also stems from the fact that so many polling organizations (including many in-house polling operations within news media companies) now exist. Gallup, Harris, Ipsos, Pew Research, Zogby, Roper, and Rasmussen are among the most notable polling organizations, while other notable polls include those undertaken by NBC News/*Wall Street Journal*, CBS/*New York Times*, CNN/Opinion Research, *USA Today*, and Quinnipiac University. Various political websites also provide aggregate polling results, such as RealClearPolitics. These aggregate polls combine the results of other polls about election outcomes to provide a larger sample.

Political analysts emphasize, however, that some polls are much more reliable than others. America's shift toward cell phones and away from landlines has made it more difficult, more time-consuming, and much more expensive for pollsters to reach a true random sample of Americans. The FCC forbids automatic dialing of cell phones, and with traditional landlines no longer dominant in American households, response rates have fallen dramatically. In addition, many polls now have smaller sample sizes, which make them statistically unreliable, or rely on "registered" as opposed to "likely" voters. This inaccuracy was underscored in dramatic fashion in 2016, when most pollsters and election forecasters confidently predicted that Hillary Clinton would defeat Donald Trump. On Election Day, Clinton was a heavy favorite to win, with forecasts claiming 70–99 percent certainty. Various factors caused the inaccuracies, including nonresponse bias (all demographic groups do not respond equally despite random sampling of the population), the existence of "shy Trumpers" (supporters of Trump who did not want to admit to socially "undesirable" behavior by stating their support), and inaccuracies in polling methodology to identity likely voters.

PRESIDENTIAL DEBATES

Since 1976, there have been at least two presidential debates and one vice-presidential debate (with the exception of 1980, when no vice-presidential debate occurred) during the general election campaign. For candidates, the debates enable direct outreach in a live setting. Since there is no declared winner or loser, the goal for each candidate is to clearly artic-ulate one's policy positions and political views; to convey a "presidential" demeanor; to challenge the positions, priorities, and records of his or her opponent; and to avoid committing a major gaffe. For voters, the debates offer an opportunity to see how each candidate performs under the intense pressure of a live event. The debates also represent the only time during the campaign season that both candidates answer the same questions and address each other directly. The debates are sponsored by the nonpartisan Presidential Debate Commission, which works with each campaign to negotiate such things as the style of the debate (some feature a single mod-erator, others use multiple questioners, and still others feature "town hall" events in which the candidates field questions from ordinary Americans). The Commission also determines the place, time, and duration of each debate (regarding the latter, most debates are 90 minutes in length).

Media coverage of the debates is intense, and viewing audiences are reli-ably large. More than 84 million people watched the first presidential debate between Trump and Clinton in 2016, which was 17 million more than those who watched the first debate between President Obama and Republican nominee Mitt Romney in 2012. Media sources are also active after the debate in declaring a winner; cable and network news outlets gen-erally conduct a "snap" poll after each debate to see how a sample of view-ers rated the performance of each candidate (though these polls are inaccurate as they are not as large or as randomly generated as standard public opinion polls). Some networks also use focus groups during the debate to see how viewers respond to each candidate's statements and claims. Each campaign will also have several staffers in the spin room (an area designated for media interviews with the candidate or campaign sur-rogates) following the debate to make the case to journalists that their can-didate "won" the debate; campaign surrogates also do the rounds of television news shows immediately following each debate to advocate for their candidate's "winning" performance. Often, a particular line or phrase from a debate will generate more news than specific policy statements. For example, Trump referred to Clinton as a "nasty woman" during the third debate in 2016, setting off worldwide media attention, particularly on social media. Debates, however, are not the game changers that news media organizations make them out to be. Although missteps by a candi-date or a lackluster performance by an incumbent president or candidate can temporarily shift public opinion, most scholars assert that historically presidential debates have had little if any effect on the election outcome.

RUNNING MATES

Various considerations go into the selection of a running mate, yet the actual event of announcing the vice-presidential candidate often ends up being anticlimactic. The main goal is to "balance the ticket" with the selection. This means that the choice for vice president is often selected with an eye toward finding someone with perceived strengths that can help neutralize potential weaknesses of the presidential candidate, whether in terms of political experience, geography, or ideological appeal within the party. For example, if a presidential candidate knows that he or she is publicly perceived (or treated by the media) as extremely conservative or progressive, the campaign may decide to select a vice presidential nominee with a moderate reputation.

Selecting one's running mate requires an intense vetting process. It often includes a committee of party and campaign leaders who participate in creating the short list, and their search and vetting process typically spurs weeks of breathless speculation from news media. Yet little evidence exists to suggest that running mates add to or detract from how the presidential candidate is viewed by voters. In recent presidential campaigns, women politicians have regularly made the short list of potential running mates, yet as of early 2020, only three women—Democrats Geraldine Ferraro in 1984 and Kamala Harris in 2020 Republican Sarah Palin in 2008—have been nominated for vice president by a major political party.

CONCLUSION

Though the Electoral College votes will not be cast until December of the election year, and will not be officially counted during a joint session of Congress until a few weeks later in early January, for all intents and purposes, the final act in the presidential selection process occurs on Election Night when news media organizations declare a winner. By that time, American voters would have endured a long and at times complicated process marked by blizzards of fundraising requests, campaign ads, public opinion polls, media appearances, get-out-the-vote efforts, and strategizing by campaign consultants.

It is important to remember, however, that the skills that are needed to win a presidential campaign do not necessarily equate with the skills that will be necessary to govern. Newly elected presidents have roughly

11 weeks between the Election Day and their inauguration to transition from candidate to chief executive, which leaves little time for them to celebrate their electoral victory. Cabinet and other political appointments must be made, legislative agendas must be formulated, and strategies must shift from campaigning in swing states to governing within a system of three coequal branches. The coalition of voters who elect a president is not the same coalition that will be needed to successfully govern, as presidents must contend with members of Congress; the federal judiciary; state officials; foreign dignitaries; and any number of federal, state, and local bureaucrats when attempting to create and enforce national policies. As the remaining chapters will show, getting elected may seem easier in hindsight once presidents are faced with the many political and policy challenges they will confront while in residence at 1600 Pennsylvania Avenue.

3

The President and the American Public

Public popularity and charismatic speaking skills are not qualities that the framers of the Constitution viewed as important for presidents. In fact, the fear of a tyrannical monarch, combined with the desire to isolate the presidency from the popular will of voters (through the Electoral College) led to the design of an office that left little room for connection between the president and the American public. Yet, as with other aspects of the office, dramatic changes have occurred in how presidents use the public aspects of the office. Aided by expanding media technologies and capabilities, several presidents throughout the twentieth century have institutionalized the president's role in attempting to use public support to lead and govern. How presidents communicate—and to whom and where—is now a top strategic priority as the White House tries to manage and control the president's public image and shape news coverage and public opinion.

This chapter considers the various aspects of the public presidency and how those have changed the presidents' attempt to govern. The rise of the rhetorical presidency at the turn of the twentieth century connected presidents to the American public in ways that advanced perceptions of the president as the symbolic leader of the nation, despite the fact that the framers' design of three coequal branches had not been altered. Communication strategies are now an essential part of the day-to-day operation of the White House. While some presidents are skilled communicators who perform well with major speeches and other public events, not all presidents have the skill set to successfully govern from center stage. Two critical factors in the extent of success a president can have in controlling the political agenda include presidential rhetoric and the president's relationship with the news media. These factors contribute to a president's public approval rating, which can shape the political environment in which a president seeks to push his legislative agenda. Though public popularity (or lack thereof) is but one component of that political environment, the information and imagery provided by ever-expanding media technology dominates the American political process of which the president has emerged as a leading character.

THE RHETORICAL PRESIDENCY

What is meant by a rhetorical presidency? In general, it has been described as the way presidents use rhetorical skills to advance their policy priorities and broader ideological objectives. Several scholars argue that the presidency as an institution was transformed into a "rhetorical presidency" during the early part of the twentieth century. The current political culture now demands the president to be a popular leader, and with that comes the duty for holders of the office to publicly promote policy initiatives, defend themselves and their political party, and shepherd the American public through good times and bad. In doing so, however, the presidency has now greatly deviated from the original constitutional intentions of the framers, removing the buffer between citizens and their representatives. Presidential rhetoric is a means for mobilizing the masses, and it is a primary tool used by presidents in their attempts to implement policy objectives. That does not mean that presidents are always successful in their attempts to do this, but it has nonetheless become a permanent feature of how presidents attempt to govern.

This trend began with presidents William McKinley (1897–1901), Theodore Roosevelt (1901–1909), and Woodrow Wilson (1913–1921), as all three relied on public speaking tours and press coverage to garner support for their policy agendas. Roosevelt was especially influential as he used the "bully pulpit"—the Oval Office—to engage in a public dialogue with citizens. Roosevelt used his rhetorical skills to increase the power of the presidency by consciously enlisting the support of the public. This stance was in alignment with his view of the presidency itself—that he was the steward of the people and that weak presidential leadership during the nineteenth century had left the American system of government open to the harmful influence of special interests.

Roosevelt's actions increased the public's expectation of both the president and the office. Some presidential scholars view the expansion of the public presidency as a positive institutional and constitutional feature, as well as one imagined by the framers as a necessary element of a properly functioning republic. Others, however, view this shift as a dangerous expansion of presidential power and in conflict with what the framers had in mind, since many spoke out about the risks of having a popular leader or demagogue in the office of the presidency. Regardless, this has caused an institutional dilemma; the president now fulfills popular functions and serves the nation through mass appeal, even as the presidency has deviated from the original constitutional intention of the framers by removing the buffer between citizens and their representative in the White House.

While most presidents after Roosevelt have followed his lead in elevating the power of the presidency by positioning themselves as the spokesperson for the American public, not all have enjoyed success with the public aspects of the office. Through his public leadership, Wilson, especially during World War I, established the presidency as a strong position of leadership at both the national and international levels. He used his rhetorical skills to promote many progressive policy initiatives and embarked on a national whistle-stop railroad tour in an ultimately unsuccessful bid to gain support for U.S. entry into the League of Nations. The emergence of several new communications technologies after his presidency, however, accelerated the emergence of the rhetorical presidency.

Radio was the first mass communication technology to aid presidents in their public efforts. Franklin D. Roosevelt (1933–1945) relied heavily on radio broadcasts in his efforts to persuade the American public to support his New Deal policies during the 1930s and American involvement in World War II during the early 1940s. Roosevelt delivered the first of his 30 so-called fireside chats—national radio broadcasts—at the end of his first week in office in March 1933. Roosevelt used this first broadcast to reassure the American public, in simple, understandable language, that he would guide the national economy out of the Great Depression and into recovery. This began an effective trend on which Roosevelt would rely throughout his time in office—the use of radio to enter the living rooms of Americans to talk about the problems and challenges facing the country. His successor, Harry Truman (1945–1953), used radio with even more frequency as the medium, and its presence around the globe rapidly increased.

The public aspects of the office took on an even greater importance for presidents with the start of the television age. The rapid expansion of television during the 1950s occurred while Dwight Eisenhower (1953–1961) occupied the White House. Eisenhower became the first president to utilize television as a means to communicate with the American public, and his administration became much more visible than any other before it through the use of filmed press conferences, televised cabinet meetings, and televised fireside chats. Yet the true potential of television as a governing tool would not be realized until the presidencies of John F. Kennedy (1961–1963) and Ronald Reagan (1981–1989). Both became known for their frequent use of television to delivery inspiring and eloquent speeches about public policy and their visions for the country.

Kennedy used television to talk of a "New Frontier" (the term he used to describe his domestic and national agenda to inspire Americans) and motivated many Americans to become active in public service. Kennedy and his advisors saw the medium of television as an excellent governing tool for the president to expand his influence and power over national politics. By the mid-1960s, when Lyndon B. Johnson occupied the Oval Office (he succeeded Kennedy after the latter was assassinated in November 1963), the president had become a central focus of news from Washington, and the ability to help shape public opinion through televised speeches and press conferences began to provide the president an important advantage during the legislative process. Two decades later, Reagan also saw the bully pulpit as one of the president's most important tools. He used skills acquired from his pre-politics career as an actor to project what his supporters regarded as a strong image of leadership that restored their faith in government. Reagan also successfully and strategically managed his time on television. For example, he held few press conferences, but they were televised during prime time for maximum coverage. In addition, his White House communications team understood the value of consistency in messaging (by speaking in one voice throughout the administration on policies, they often had success in shaping news coverage to the president's advantage). The presidents in between Kennedy and Reagan—Lyndon Johnson (1963–1969), Richard Nixon (1969–1974), Gerald Ford (1974–1977), and Jimmy Carter (1977–1981), as well as Reagan's successor George H. W. Bush (1989–1993) also used television in myriad ways, but none seemed to master the use of television to cultivate a strong and positive image with the American public.

Dramatic technological changes also transformed American politics and the presidency itself during the 1990s. It was during this time that presidents began contending with 24-hour news coverage on cable television networks as well as the arrival of the Internet as a new communications medium. While presidents found new opportunities to connect with the American public, challenges also emerged as the style and tone of political news coverage became more critical and negative. Bill Clinton (1993–2001), the first baby boomer president raised during the television age, often relied on alternative television opportunities or "new media" talk shows and live town hall meetings to bypass the traditional Washington press corps and speak directly to the American people. But while those unconventional approaches worked well for Clinton by giving him more options to deliver his message unfiltered to the audience, expanding mediums and technology also adversely affected the leadership potential for presidents.

During the George W. Bush (2001–2009) presidency, the political environment continued to be shaped by the increased competition among more and more news outlets, as well as newer and ever-expanding technological advancements. This time period was marked by many changes in the news industry as online news sources became more dominant and traditional "legacy" outlets (such as print newspapers and magazines and commercial broadcast network news) downsized, lost influence, or went out of business due to declining levels of both customers and advertisers. This left news more fragmented and targeted at smaller audiences, and it created a dynamic in which fewer Americans got their news from the same sources. This trend was further exacerbated by the rise of hyper-partisan news outlets on television, in print, and online. Moreover, smart phones, streaming services, and other digital entertainment options offered a multitude of other distractions for Americans. These developments posed many challenges for presidents and administrations seeking to maintain control over their public image and policy message. In such a saturated media environment, it has become more difficult for presidents to command the attention of the American public.

Social media platforms have also become a dominant force in presidential communication. Barack Obama (2009–2017) had a strong presence on social media with Facebook, Twitter, and Instagram accounts, while the White House also had Twitter and Snapchat accounts. In fact, by the time Obama left office in January 2017, Obama had 80.4 million followers on Twitter (@BarackObama), while the White House had 13.2 million followers (@WhiteHouse) and @POTUS had 13.4 million followers. Donald Trump (2017–present), who relied heavily on Twitter to reach out to voters during the 2016 presidential election, entered the White House with more than 22 million followers on Twitter (@realDonaldTrump), and that number had increased to more than 72 million by the start of 2020.

WHITE HOUSE COMMUNICATION STRATEGIES

Managing the rhetorical aspects of the presidency continues to be an evolving challenge for presidents and their advisors regarding harnessing available technology and the public expectations of the office. As such, presidents now must develop extensive communication strategies along with their legislative agendas and various other day-to-day responsibilities. A communication strategy incorporates the leadership style of the president with a wide array of communication components including presidential rhetoric and speechwriting, presidential public activities, the presidential policy agenda, and the presidential-press relationship. An effective presidential communication strategy can be a critical factor in developing and implementing the administration's policy goals. Presidential rhetoric has changed over time as media technologies have continued to expand, providing citizens with more in-depth coverage of the president. Due especially to visual and online coverage, presidential advisers now develop communication strategies that seek more support for the president as a person or leader and less support for specific policy proposals. This has led to an emphasis on symbolic and ceremonial, rather than deliberative (as in policy specific), speech.

In addition, the television age of politics also brought with it the "going public" strategy, which assumes that a president can gain public support for his policy agenda by speaking directly to the American people through national addresses and other high-profile media appearances. Evidence suggests that this strategy is not always effective in shaping or moving public opinion in a president's favor, however. Not only can the president's voice be easily drowned out, but Americans are not as attentive to the national news as they once were. As political parties have become more polarized, media sources more fragmented, and entertainment options more numerous, presidents now sometimes choose to "go local" (such as doing interviews with local media outlets) as opposed to "going national" in their public strategies to gain support from the base of their parties, select interest groups, and voters in key areas as, for example, an address to the nation does not carry the same significance that it once did.

The president relies on two groups of advisors within the White House to control his public image and that of his administration—the Press Office and the Office of Communications. The press secretary heads the press office and is responsible for preparing press releases, coordinating news and holding daily press briefings for the White House press corps (though these no longer occur regularly in the Trump White House), and interacting with reporters who cover the president. The press secretary also serves as an important public spokesperson for the president and as a liaison between reporters and the White House. The Office of Communications, created in 1969 during Richard Nixon's (1969–1974) presidency, develops a long-term public relations strategy and coordinates presidential coverage in regional and local media outlets.

Speech writing is also an integral part of White House communication strategies. Major public addresses, particularly the State of the Union and major policy speeches, set the president's legislative agenda for both the public and Congress. Major addresses and other public appearances are used by administrations to sell each president's agenda and policy preferences to the public, the news media, and other lawmakers and public officials.

Some early presidents relied on the help of others to write their speeches, most notably George Washington, Andrew Jackson, and Andrew Johnson, but most wrote their own. Thomas Jefferson, John Adams, James Madison, and Abraham Lincoln were all known for eloquent and effective speeches they authored themselves. By the twentieth century, the public leadership strategies and the increased attention placed on public addresses by Theodore Roosevelt and Woodrow Wilson gave rise to the need for permanent speechwriters within the White House. Warren G. Harding (1921–1923) hired the first official White House speechwriter, journalist Judson Welliver, who maintained a low public profile. When Franklin D. Roosevelt entered the White House, presidential speeches became more of a collaborative effort between the president, his advisors, and his speechwriters. Other presidents, most notably Kennedy, Nixon, Reagan, Clinton, and Obama, were also extensively involved in the writing and phraseology of their major public addresses.

Presidents now rely heavily on public events as an essential component of governing; a steady increase has occurred in the number of public events, particularly the use of major public addresses, since the start of the 1980s. This can be attributed to the influence and expansion of television and online coverage, changes in the political environment that have encouraged presidents to go public more often, and each president's public leadership style. It is not surprising that while expanding technologies allowed an increase in the amount and type of White House coverage, the president's schedule of public events also increased.

TRADITIONAL MAJOR PUBLIC ADDRESSES OF THE PRESIDENT

While presidents since the start of the television age have relied on various public strategies to publicize their policy agendas and to improve their standing with the American public, there are certain major public addresses that are required and expected of every president. The best known of these speeches are the inaugural address and the annual State of the Union address.

The inaugural address is given by the president shortly after he or takes the oath of office. Presidents typically see the inaugural address as an opportunity to set the tone for their time in office with the public, other political actors, and even the news media. It is also an opportunity for them to talk about broader political principles and not specific policies.

Some of the most memorable and quoted inaugural addresses have occurred during times of great national crisis, such as Abraham Lincoln's address in 1861 (often remembered for the "better nature of our angels" line at the end of the speech) or Franklin D. Roosevelt's first inaugural address in 1933 (when he told Depression-stunned Americans that "the only thing we have to fear is fear itself"). Other presidents, such as Kennedy in 1961 ("ask not what your country can do for you" and "the torch has been passed to a new generation of Americans") and Reagan in 1981 ("government is not the solution to our problem; government *is* the problem"), were skilled public speakers and used the inaugural address to present a recurring theme for their presidencies.

The president's annual State of the Union address is perhaps the most anticipated and analyzed of all presidential speeches. Article II section 3 of the U.S. Constitution requires that the president "shall from time to time give to the Congress information on the state of the Union and recommend to their consideration such measures as he shall judge necessary and expedient," but there is no requirement that the president give this information in an address to a joint session of Congress. Both George Washington (1789–1797) and John Adams (1797–1801) gave an address to Congress in addition to submitting a written report. For presidents Thomas Jefferson (1801–1809) through William Howard Taft (1909–1913), this constitutional requirement was met by only submitting a written report to the Congress on the state of the union. Woodrow Wilson (1913–1921) revived the practice of delivering an address to Congress, which has continued most every year since.

Traditionally delivered near the start of the calendar year, the State of the Union address is not only a report to Congress on the actual "state" of the union but also a statement of the president's proposed policy agenda for the upcoming year. This has evolved as a unique opportunity for presidents, in upholding their constitutional duty, to remind both the audience in attendance (Congress) and those watching and listening at home (the public) of the president's role in shaping the national agenda. In recent decades, the State of the Union address has involved an extensive White House communications and media strategy plan for events prior to, on the day of, and after the actual speech. The goal is to try to maximize the impact of the president's speech in terms of both his policy agenda and his standing with the American public.

Other major policy addresses are also expected of the president, including televised addresses to the nation in times of crisis or national urgency (usually involving national tragedy, U.S. military action, natural disasters, or economic crises). Presidents also occasionally deliver policy addresses with the expectation of national news coverage (usually delivered before a large group such as a national convention for an interest group or a university graduation). While a major policy address by itself demands much attention from White House staffers in various offices (including speechwriting, press, media affairs), the ancillary events that go along with a major policy address (press conferences, presidential and surrogate interviews, photo ops, speech distribution, and other advance work) also play a large role in the communications strategy for a specific presidential speech.

THE PRESIDENTIAL-PRESS RELATIONSHIP

The news media have always been among the most influential political actors with whom presidents must contend. The relationship is often an adversarial one since the president and news media need each other yet have different goals—the president wants positive coverage about the actions and policies of his administration, but big stories or breaking news for the press usually come from negative and scandal-oriented stories about the president or his administration. Rarely has a president not complained about the news media, the White House press corps, or the nature and quality of the coverage received. The press, however, plays an important role as a watchdog of the government with a responsibility to inform the American people. This mission often puts reporters at odds with the White House.

The relationship between the president and the American press has a long and colorful history. American newspapers during the late 18th and early 19th centuries were highly partisan in both their political loyalties and coverage of events in Washington. By the mid-nineteenth century, with advanced printing capabilities and a desire to provide more objective news coverage for increasing circulations, newspapers began to cover the White House as a formal beat. News coverage of the presidency dramatically increased during the administration of Theodore Roosevelt, who cultivated positive press coverage to maintain strong ties to the American public. Since then, with the rise of the rhetorical presidency and the continual expansion of media technology, presidents have increasingly relied on the press to communicate their vision to both the American public and other important political actors.

The White House press corps first received working space within the White House during the administration of Theodore Roosevelt. He included press quarters within the new West Wing of the White House when it was built in 1904. Ten years later, the White House Correspondents' Association was formed. This organization of journalists contributed to the trend of professionalization of reporters within the newspaper industry during the early part of the twentieth century. The White House press corps experienced tremendous growth during the 1930s and 1940s as presidential influence over national politics increased under the New Deal programs. The emergence of the television age during the 1950s, and its expansive growth during the 1960s and 1970s, greatly contributed to the growth in size of the White House press corps. Other contributing factors include the increased importance and size of the federal government and the role it plays in the lives of individuals, which requires reporters from non-Washington media outlets to cover policymaking at the national level. Today, approximately 1,700 people hold White House press credentials, though not all are considered "regulars" on the White House beat.

The prominence of the White House beat has also increased within the journalism industry and is now viewed as a premier assignment in most news organizations. The reporters who regularly cover the White House include representatives from a variety of legacy and new media outlets, including the top daily newspapers (*New York Times, Washington Post, Los Angeles Times, Wall Street Journal, USA Today*), the major networks (*ABC, CBS, NBC, Fox, CNN, MSNBC*), and wire services (*Associated Press, United Press International, Reuters*). In recent years, with the growth of Internet news sources, reporters from online sources such as *Politico, Huffington Post*, and *Townhall*, to name a few, are also regulars within the White House press room. The growth in the size of the White House press corps has also contributed to the expansion of both the White House Press Office and Office of Communications to handle the increased needs and demands of Washington reporters.

Press conferences provide the president with an opportunity to make news by formally interacting with the White House press corps. Press conferences have become an institutionalized tradition in which all presidents are expected to participate. A written transcript is kept of all questions and answers, and most presidents begin the session with a prepared opening statement. Since they were first televised live in the 1960s, press conferences are often less about informing reporters and the public about important issues and more about controlling the president's public image. Theodore Roosevelt held some of the earliest press conferences, scheduling informal sessions with members of the press on Sundays so they could file stories that the president wished to highlight from Washington in Monday's newspapers. Taft was the first president to hold regular press conferences. These occurred twice a week until he stopped the practice after what he described as "an unfortunate session" with aggressive reporters. Wilson, Harding, Coolidge, and Hoover (until the onset of the Depression) returned to the practice of regular press conferences, usually twice weekly, and formal events. Each also required reporters to submit their questions in advance.

Franklin D. Roosevelt changed that requirement, as well as the formal setting for press conferences. He had frequent and informal meetings with reporters in the Oval Office, and he held a total of 881 press conferences, a yearly average of approximately 70. He was famous for his congenial personality toward the press and his "off-the-record" remarks. Using these tools as well as his famous radio "fireside chats," Roosevelt proved himself a master at news management who helped shape many headlines throughout the nation's newspapers over his many years in office. Truman averaged 38 press conferences per year. He returned press conferences to more formal affairs and moved the location in 1950 out of the Oval Office and into the Executive Office Building. Truman and his advisors began to exercise more control over the content and structure of press conferences, relying on pre-conference briefings and an increased use of prepared opening statements.

Eisenhower was the first president to encounter television cameras during a press conference, and he allowed taping for later television release. His successor, John F. Kennedy, was innovative with his groundbreaking use of live televised press conferences, which both the press and public found entertaining. Lyndon B. Johnson could never match the Kennedy style during press conferences, and the inaccurate reports of American progress in winning the Vietnam War that he delivered during these events contributed to his declining popularity as that war dragged on. The frequency of press conferences dropped during Nixon's presidency. Nixon and his advisors believed that the mystique of the presidency could be maintained through limited public appearances, but Nixon also was famously disdainful of the press. He averaged only seven press conferences per year during his presidency. Presidents Ford and Carter both attempted to restore credibility to the White House and its relationship with the press after Nixon's resignation by increasing the number of press conferences after the Nixon years. Both used these opportunities to speak bluntly to the press about the problems facing the nation in the mid-to-late 1970s. While neither received high marks for style during press conferences, both Ford and Carter were known for their substantive knowledge of government policies.

While his public skills earned him the nickname the "Great Communicator," Reagan held fewer press conferences than even Nixon did, averaging just less than six per year. This was due to primarily Reagan's habit of making misstatements and verbal gaffes during unscripted give-and-take interactions with reporters. President George H.W. Bush (1989–1993) held more press conferences than Reagan and also began the practice of holding joint press conferences with foreign leaders. Bush afforded the press extensive access to the entire administration; he hoped to gain favorable coverage by holding many informal discussions with reporters, and he courted the press as members of the political elite. Clinton continued the practice of holding joint press conferences with foreign leaders (a trend that continued with George W. Bush and Obama), but he did not hold many formal press conferences, particularly during his second term (due in part to his impeachment in 1998). During his first three years in office,

Trump held few formal press conferences, but he did hold impromptu question-and-answer sessions with reporters at other times. The Trump administration also stopped holding daily press briefings hosted by the press secretary. From that point forward, the chief means by which the Trump White House communicated with the public was through Trump's personal Twitter account.

In the post-Watergate years, press coverage of the president and the White House has become more personal, intrusive, and obsessed with scandal. Coverage of national politics, and in particular the presidency, has not only personalized and politicized the functioning of the national government, but the immediacy of cable news and online coverage has also accelerated the decision-making process for presidents. Americans have come to expect that the personal lives of presidents will make news, which has also desensitized the public to the tabloid-style reporting about personal indiscretions. Presidents must now pay close attention to their image as it is portrayed in media, but determining what is good for the president in terms of control over the message may not be the same as substantive information about the political process for the American electorate.

Presidents have always attempted to exert control over news coverage, fully aware that their administration's fortunes often depend to a great extent on how the press portrays it and its policies. While presidents can usually enjoy some measure of deference from the press in terms of coverage during times of crisis or certain ceremonial occasions, usually reporters place presidential actions within a political context—in other words, they ascribe political motives and implications to every decision that a president makes, just as they do for other political figures in Congress and elsewhere.

PUBLIC OPINION

Public approval plays an important role in a president's effectiveness as a leader and success as a policymaker, as high approval ratings can translate into more successful dealings with Congress. The press and its expectations of presidential performance also influence this. Some scholars claim that polls are misleading and nothing but a "ratings race." Americans are conditioned, especially through media coverage, to view their leader as "the president," not part of the institution of the presidency, making him an independent and unique symbol of power for the U.S. government.

Presidents enter office with high public expectations, which often cannot be met. Circumstances can play an important role in popularity, including broad economic trends, international events, and scandals in various corners of the administration—factors over which a president may have little or no control. Most polls focus on whether voters approve of the president's job performance, but factors such as perceived likability of the president and the overall state of the nation inevitably influence responses. Consider Bill Clinton's approval rating in 1998. In the middle of being impeached over personal misconduct, his approval rating throughout the year remained in the 60 percent range; Americans became good at compartmentalizing as they disapproved of Clinton's personal behavior yet were satisfied with the strong economy. In addition, political scientists point out that in modern America's politically polarized environment—one in which large numbers of voters describe themselves as strongly liberal or conservative and presidential elections are typically close and fiercely contested—it is difficult for presidents to achieve widespread popularity.

Regular tracking of the public's view of the president and his job performance began in 1945 during the Truman administration, when the Gallup poll first asked members of the American public if they approved of the president's job performance. According to Gallup, from 1945 through 2020, the average presidential approval rating is 53 percent. Of the 13 presidents Gallup has tracked since 1945, only six averaged approval ratings above 50 percent over the course of their presidencies, including Eisenhower (65 percent), Kennedy (70 percent), Johnson (55 percent), Reagan (53 percent), George H. W. Bush (61 percent), and Clinton (55 percent). But every president experiences peaks and valleys in approval rating. For example, Obama's average approval in the Gallup polls over his two terms was 47.9 percent, but his final job approval rating was 59 percent. Meanwhile, the highest poll ratings ever recorded by Gallup belonged to George H. W. Bush (89 percent in February 1991 during the Gulf War) and George W. Bush (90 percent in the days following the terrorist attacks of 9/11). Often, such high approval ratings are attributed to what scholars refer to as a "rally 'round the flag" effect, which means that American citizens show short-term support for the president in a time of national or international crisis. Typically, however, this surge in support is only temporary. In fact, George H.W. Bush lost his bid for reelection only 20 months after posting his 89 percent approval rating.

Trump is unique as he became the first president inaugurated with an approval rating below 50 percent on the day he took office. As of early 2020, his highest recorded approval rating has been 49 percent with an average of 40 percent (the latter is the lowest of any president). Citizens often form lasting impressions of presidential candidates that continue into their presidencies if elected. In Trump's case, in 2016 he was considered the least popular presidential candidate in the history of public opinion polling. But he was able to eke out a narrow victory in the Electoral College because his opponent, Democratic nominee Hillary Clinton, was the second least popular candidate in polling history.

CONCLUSION

While the public presidency is not discussed within the U.S. Constitution, it is difficult to imagine a president shunning the public responsibilities now associated with the job. White House communication strategies are extensive and multifaceted; advisors must consider the president's strengths and weaknesses in deciding when and where to hold events, give speeches, grant interviews, and how best to craft the administration's narrative within a hyper-partisan and competitive political news environment. Not only is the political environment constantly in flux thanks to rapidly changing media technology but also public opinion about the president and various policy decisions can also shift quickly thanks to instantaneous news coverage that goes viral on social media. Managing the public aspects of the job is just one of many skills that presidents and their advisors need to be successful at, but presidents who are strong communicators and can adapt to changes in the news industry have a distinct advantage over their political rivals.

4

The President and the Legislative Branch

Presidents discover fairly soon after taking office that the skills that helped get them elected are much different from the skills it takes to govern effectively. This is perhaps most apparent in the president's relationship with Congress. As the most representative of the three branches of government, it was no accident that the framers outlined the legislative branch in Article I of the Constitution. The legislative process begins with Congress, and the role of its members is clear. Yet the public also expects the president to provide legislative leadership. For the president, the job of legislating and administering public policies requires talents of persuasion, personal and organizational leadership, and managerial skills that can move a cumbersome and complex government to get things done. Moreover, Congress is a formidable institutional force in its own right. As President John F. Kennedy said in a December 17, 1962, interview in the Oval Office, "The fact is I think the Congress looks more powerful sitting here than it did when I was there in the Congress. But that is because when you are in Congress you are one of a hundred in the Senate or one of 435 in the House, so that the power is so divided. But from here I look at a Congress, and I look at the collective power of the Congress, particularly the bloc action, and it is a substantial power."

This chapter considers the constitutional role that presidents play in the legislative process, which goes beyond simply signing or vetoing bills. When seeking to enact a legislative agenda, presidents face several potential sources of conflict with Congress, given the system of checks and balances outlined in the Constitution. Various factors can come into play, including the balance of power between Democrats and Republicans in Washington, D.C., as well as the president's ability to work with leaders from his own party as well as those from across the aisle.

CONSTITUTIONAL POWERS

Article I Section 1 gives Congress "all the legislative powers herein granted," and unlike the few enumerated (explicitly mentioned) powers listed for the president in Article II, Article I Section 8 provides a detailed list of Congress' enumerated powers, including the power to declare war, regulate commerce, regulate the military, and issue currency. This section of the Constitution also includes a "necessary and proper" clause granting Congress inherent powers (that is, governing responsibilities related to the specific powers granted). Constitutional experts agree that the framers expected Congress to have primary responsibility for legislative action and that the president's role in that sphere would be minor.

While the president does have some formal legislative powers, the list is brief. They include the power to call Congress into special session (though this is much less important now as Congress stays in session most of the year), the requirement to provide a state of the union message to Congress, as well as a budget message and economic report (which is seen as a way to announce to the nation the president's policy goals), the ability to recommend legislation to Congress (which not only grants the president the power to call attention to issues but also encourages Congress to pay attention to the president since it is mandated by the Constitution), and the power to sign bills into law or to veto bills of which he or she disapproves.

Throughout much of the nineteenth century, Congress served as the dominant branch of government. However, presidents began to take a more active role in the legislative process in the early twentieth century in response to industrialization and urbanization trends that were rapidly changing American society. Theodore Roosevelt and Woodrow Wilson were both responsible for expanding presidential power in this area. Wilson took the lead in defining goals of his administration to Congress, helping formulate bills, reinstating the practice abandoned in 1796 of personally delivering the State of the Union address to Congress, using cabinet members to build coalitions with Congress, and personally lobbying for support of his programs on Capitol Hill. Ironically, Wilson had been a student of Congress long before he ever moved into the White House. While working on his PhD in political science in the 1880s, he wrote *Congressional Government: A Study in American Politics* (1885), which examines the structure of Congress and how executive officials must follow the dictates of the legislature.

Franklin D. Roosevelt greatly expanded not only the size of the executive branch but also the influence of the president over the legislative process in Congress. The Truman and Eisenhower administrations continued this trend and institutionalized the legislative role by creating structures and processes to assist in carrying out this role, such as using White House staff to lobby and coordinate the legislative agenda.

While the powers of Congress expanded during the twentieth century in terms of the subjects on which it legislates, its influence as an innovator of public policy has greatly declined. For presidents, congressional support must be carefully cultivated and maintained, and when the conditions that created it change, it can rapidly decrease. When presidents have this support, they are viewed as productive and in charge of government. When it wanes or disappears—which can happen quickly—they run the risk of being viewed as weak and ineffectual.

DIVIDED GOVERNMENT

Gridlock (which means that policies are not easily approved due to competing governing philosophies and priorities in Washington) is a prominent feature of the American system of government, yet it is one of the aspects of politics that American citizens dislike the most. Is government gridlock what the framers intended? The framers were fearful of political factions and the ability of popular opinion to take over governmental policies. They wanted a president who was not monarchical and did not have a lot of power. They also wanted a system of shared powers between the three branches, with each branch having the ability to resist the encroachment of the others. As a result, the American system of government is based on incrementalism, which means that policy changes occur slowly. Dramatic, sweeping reforms are thus rare, which provides more stability to the system of government. The slower reaction time and the existence of checks and balances provide for more deliberation among the three branches.

Party politics plays a large role in the president's relationship with Congress, so not only does the legislative branch maintain checks and balances against the president but also does the balance of political power within Congress. Presidents typically enjoy better relations with Congress when the president's party also controls (through holding a majority of the seats) both the House of Representatives and the Senate. However, "divided government," in which the president's opposing party controls one or both chambers, occurs regularly. Since 1832, after reforms to the Electoral College moved the nomination of presidential candidates from congressional caucuses to party conventions, the United States has experienced divided government roughly 40 percent of the time. Divided government has been even more common in recent decades. Since 1952, voters have chosen a unified government—one in which the president and majorities in both houses of Congress are from the same party—in only 13 out of 34 presidential election years (1952, 1960, 1962, 1964, 1966, 1976, 1978, 1992, 2000, 2002, 2004, 2008, and 2016). And even these state of affairs can be relatively brief. In the 2018 midterm elections, for example, President Trump and his fellow Republicans lost their unified hold on the Oval Office and Congress when Democrats won a majority in the House of Representatives.

It is also important to remember that other factors can come into play beyond whether government is unified or divided. When it comes to working together with Congress to pass legislation, presidents are either helped or crippled by other factors such as the state of the economy, whether America is at war, and the existence of other domestic or international tensions. Major political events can shape a president's ability to pass legislation as well. For example, following John F. Kennedy's assassination in 1963, Lyndon Johnson pushed through major pieces of legislation, including the Civil Rights Act of 1964, in part as a tribute to Kennedy. Following the political scandal of Watergate and Richard Nixon's resignation in 1974, Congress passed major reforms in such areas as ethics and campaign financing. Finally, not only has split-ticket voting contributed to the frequency of divided government (which means that voters choose a president and members of Congress from different parties), but presidents are also not always able to count on party loyalty in their negotiations with Congress on key administration priorities and initiatives.

SOURCES OF CONFLICT

Many sources of conflict exist in the presidential-congressional relationship when it comes to governing. First of all, the president represents a national constituency, while the 535 members of Congress represent constituencies that vary in geographical area, population, economic structure, and social composition. Individually, members of Congress are beholden to their constituents, yet as a body they must represent the nation. Both interests, especially when considering reelection efforts, are sometimes conflicting. The only way the national interest emerges in Congress is through bargaining between members and blocs of members responsive to particular interests. This practice results in the formation of temporary majority coalitions to pass specific legislation. As a result, action taken by Congress is usually reactive.

The president has a much easier time acting on behalf of the nation's interests. Divided government adds to the conflictual relationship between the two branches and usually limits the potential for social gain through public policy, but several studies suggest that progress can still be made on the policy agenda under these circumstances. For example, Bill Clinton (1993–2001) enjoyed greater legislative success working with Republicans after the 1994 midterm election. During his first two years in office, while Democrats still controlled both the House and the Senate, Clinton failed in nearly all of his major legislative goals, including health care reform, welfare reform, and campaign finance reform. But after Republicans won control of both houses for the first time in 40 years in 1994, Clinton, a moderate Democrat, had an easier time moving to the center and working with Republican leaders than he had attempting to work with the more liberal leadership within the Democratic Party. Clinton also successfully relied on a strategy known as triangulation, which meant that he embraced policies on issues such as welfare reform that occupied a middle ground between conservatives and liberals. This moderate approach produced aspects of the policy that both sides liked, and it allowed Clinton to take credit for brokering the deal.

The presidential veto is also a source of conflict between the executive and legislative branches. The president's power to sign or veto bills is found in Article 1, Section 7: "Every Bill which shall have passed the House of Representatives and the Senate, shall, before it become a Law, be presented to the President of the United States; If he approve he shall sign it, but if not he shall return it, with his Objections to that House in which it shall have originated, who shall enter the Objections at large on their Journal, and proceed to reconsider it. If after such Reconsideration two thirds of that House shall agree to pass the Bill, it shall be sent, together with the Objections, to the other House, by which it shall likewise be reconsidered, and if approved by two thirds of that House, it shall become a Law."

This is the basic process of how a bill becomes a law. Each chamber of Congress votes on the same bill, and if it passes in both the Senate and House of Representatives, it then goes to the president for his signature. Congress can override a presidential veto by a vote of two-thirds of the members in each house. The Constitution does not provide criteria for a president to judge the merit of a bill that reaches his desk. Alexander Hamilton raised the issue of why a president would veto legislation during the ratification process, arguing in *Federalist* 73 the "power to return all bills with objections to the legislature" would grant energy and strength to the presidency. However, he also argued that the "power in question has a further use. It not only serves as a shield to the executive, but it furnishes an additional security against the enaction of improper laws."

The president has 10 days (Sundays excluded) to sign or veto a bill. If the president does not sign it or return it while the legislature is in session, the bill automatically becomes law. However, if Congress is adjourned, then the bill is effectively vetoed. This "pocket veto" forces Congress to restart the legislative process, and the bill must again pass both chambers and is again subject to presidential veto. Early presidents did not rely heavily on the veto; in fact, Washington used it only twice in eight years, claiming that each law he vetoed was unconstitutional. That rationale began to change during Andrew Jackson's (1829–1837) presidency. When Jackson famously vetoed the bill to recharter the national bank in 1832, he claimed: "I sincerely regret that in the act before me I can perceive none of those modifications of the bank charter which are necessary, in my opinion, to make it compatible with justice, with sound policy, or with the Constitution of our country." Jackson contended that the individual states—not Congress—retained the power to charter, regulate, and tax corporations. Once Jackson rationalized the use of the veto on political grounds, presidents began rejecting proposed acts of Congress with more regularity.

The use of the veto as a political weapon (especially against legislation passed by the opposing party) was probably not envisioned by the framers. Many presidents, however, have used the veto not as a defense against allegedly bad legislation or Congressional encroachment on presidential authority, but as a means to protect their own legislative agendas. For example, the first six presidents vetoed a total of nine bills, and several nineteenth-century presidents—John Adams, Thomas Jefferson, John Quincy Adams, William Henry Harrison, Zachary Taylor, Millard Fillmore, and James Garfield—did not veto a single bill during their time in office. In contrast, Franklin D. Roosevelt vetoed a total of 635 bills and was overridden by Congress only nine times. These figures not only reflect his vision of presidential power but also his role and influence over the policy-making process. Presidents also use the threat of a veto as a political weapon, like when Ronald Reagan told Congress to "make my day" by raising taxes in 1985 (referencing a popular line from a 1983 Clint Eastwood movie).

While Roosevelt still holds the record of most bills vetoed (a record he holds in part because he served in office longer than any other president), other presidents have used it extensively as well. Grover Cleveland holds the record for most vetoes in a single term (414 during his first term from 1885–1889), and he used the veto another 170 times during his second term (1893–1897). During the modern era, the number of vetoes has steadily declined: Harry Truman (250), Dwight Eisenhower (181), John F. Kennedy (21), Lyndon Johnson (30), Richard Nixon (43), Gerald Ford (66),

Ronald Reagan (78), George H. W. Bush (44), Bill Clinton (37), George W. Bush (12), Barack Obama (12), and Donald Trump (6 through his first three years in office). Congress rarely overrides a presidential veto. Dating back to the Washington administration, a total of 2580 bills have been vetoed; of those, only 111 have been overridden by Congress (4% of the total) and become law.

Two other types of vetoes also exist, though both have been considered somewhat controversial by constitutional experts. The so-called legislative veto, first used in the 1930s, is a device where one or both houses of Congress passes a resolution to veto certain decisions made in the executive branch. This usually occurs to change a policy or spending by an executive agency. A legislative veto, then, is Congress allowing a president or an executive branch agency to take certain actions that may be subjected to a later approval or disapproval by one or both houses of Congress. Between 1932 and 1983, the legislative veto was used for reorganizational purposes hundreds of times and became an arrangement that worked for both the Congress and the president; presidents maintained decision-making authority they might not have otherwise, while Congress would have a second chance to weigh in on decisions. However, in 1983, in the case *INS v. Chadha*, the Supreme Court invalidated a legislative veto used to alter a decision by Immigration and Naturalization Services (an executive agency created by Congress). The Court invalidated the veto partly on the grounds that it violated Article I's "presentment requirement" (this provision means that once Congress approves a bill it must be presented to the president for approval) and partly on the grounds that it violated constitutional guarantees of separation of powers (that Congress had no right to interfere by vetoing the action of the agency). However, more than 400 legislative vetoes have been included in legislation since then. These often take the form of what are known as "report and wait" provisions that Congress will add to a bill to require congressional consultation by an executive agency before specific actions can be taken.

In 1995, Congress tried to change one aspect of the lawmaking process by approving what came to be popularly known as the "line-item veto." Following the Republican victory in the 1994 midterm elections, the new majority sought to enact a slate of campaign promises collectively known as the GOP's "Contract with America." One of those promises, championed by the new Speaker of the House Newt Gingrich (R-GA), was to create a "line-item veto" to grant the president the ability to eliminate individual items in Congressional spending bills without having to scrap the entire bill. This is a power that nearly all state governors have at their disposal, and a power that many presidents have also sought. For example, Reagan urged Congress to give him a line-item veto during his 1986 State of the Union address, arguing "we cannot win the race to the future shackled to a system that can't even pass a Federal budget." Reagan's insistence on the line-item veto came from the inability of both Congress and the White House to bring down the budget deficit and the national debt. Once the line-item veto became law in 1995 (one of the only campaign pledges in the Contract with America that actually became law), Bill Clinton became the first to use this new presidential power; he relied on the line-item veto 82 times in just 11 bills. However, the Supreme Court ruled in *Clinton v. New York* (1998) in a 7–2 decision that the line-item veto, as passed by Congress, was unconstitutional because it interfered with the separation of powers doctrine in the Constitution. The Court declared that the only way to change the power balance between the president and Congress was through passage of a constitutional amendment.

OPPORTUNITIES TO GOVERN

Despite the many sources of conflict between the president and Congress, some presidents have experienced legislative success in enacting many new policy initiatives. Perhaps the best example, and one that has set a standard difficult to match, is Franklin D. Roosevelt and the passage of his New Deal initiatives. His success can be attributed in part to the circumstances he faced upon entering office; the economic challenges of the Great Depression created a tremendous opportunity for presidential leadership—and an American public that was willing to support dramatic measures to revive the economy. In addition, Roosevelt had a strong instinct for power and what it could accomplish. After the stock market crash in 1929, Republican President Herbert Hoover had taken a hands-off approach to improving the economy, telling Americans that recovery and prosperity was just around the corner. But when Hoover's assurances that the economy would correct itself and recover failed to come to pass, Americans turned to Roosevelt, who argued for the need for robust government intervention. He defeated incumbent Hoover in 1932 by a margin of 472–59 electoral votes, and he brought with him a large majority of fellow Democrats to control both the House and the Senate. Once elected, Roosevelt believed that only dramatic presidential leadership coupled with broad powers over the national economy could save the nation and restore America's faith in political institutions.

Roosevelt's so-called New Deal included a variety of programs, reforms, regulations, and public works projects, all passed between 1933 and 1939, designed to lift the United States out of the Great Depression. The first bill that was passed into law by Roosevelt and the Democrat-controlled Congress was an emergency banking bill, which guaranteed that Americans' money in private banks would be safe. A total of 15 bills were passed by

Congress and signed by Roosevelt during his first 100 days in the White House, including legislation that created the Civilian Conservation Corps, the Federal Emergency Relief Administration, the Reconstruction Finance Corporation, and the Tennessee Valley Authority and expanded the Federal Trade Commission's regulatory powers. Other major legislation passed during Roosevelt's first term included the Social Security Act, the National Labor Relations Act, and the Works Progress Administration, all passed in 1935, bills that established the Farm Security Administration and the United States Housing Authority in 1937 and the Fair Labor Standards Act of 1938, among others.

Some of Roosevelt's New Deal legislation, especially during his first few years in office, met little resistance among the Democratic majority in Congress. However, several early pieces of legislation were struck down by the U.S. Supreme Court as unconstitutional. Despite the political realignment that benefitted the Democratic Party during the 1932 election, the Supreme Court is not beholden to partisan shifts among the electorate. All federal judges are appointed to life terms on the bench, and during Roosevelt's first term in office, seven out of the nine justices on the Supreme Court had been nominated by Republican presidents. As such, a solid majority held a more conservative approach to the expansion of the federal government. In 1935, unfavorable rulings from the Supreme Court frustrated Roosevelt so much that he considered expanding the membership of the Court by adding several justices that would see his New Deal programs and initiatives more favorably. But Roosevelt's "court-packing" plan (see discussion in chapter 5) never came to pass. He was unable to convince a majority of Democrats in Congress to increase the size of the Court to benefit his New Deal legislation. By 1937, however, the Court had shifted its stance, and this opened the door to many New Deal initiatives being upheld as constitutional. Many of the programs and agencies created during the 1930s are still in existence today.

Why did Roosevelt achieve so much legislative success? Having a large majority from his own party controlling both houses of Congress certainly helped. Roosevelt also benefitted from public perceptions that the devastation of the economic crisis merited ambitious and even radical corrective measures. In addition, Roosevelt skillfully used media of that era (especially his radio Fireside Chats) to gain the trust of the American public as a proactive leader of an extensive legislative agenda. In doing so, Roosevelt reshaped the president's role in the legislative process and created what is now known as the modern presidency. While the constitutionality of the many actions taken by Roosevelt can still be debated, historians agree that he dramatically expanded the powers of the presidency in responding to a national crisis and expanded the size and scope of the executive branch in the process.

The only other president who has come close to passing such an expansive legislative agenda since Roosevelt is Lyndon Johnson, albeit under much different circumstances. Johnson, as vice president, succeeded to the presidency on November 22, 1963, when John F. Kennedy was assassinated. Having previously served as Senate majority leader, Johnson had intimate knowledge of the legislative process and a level of political skill that few presidents have ever had. Johnson believed that constant, intense attention by the president and his administration was necessary to move his legislative program through Congress. Thanks in part to tremendous public and congressional support to finish the Kennedy policy agenda after his assassination, Johnson achieved great legislative success. He not only fulfilled some of Kennedy's top legislative priorities, he also signed into law a flurry of bills to advance what the Johnson White House termed a "Great Society." Johnson's Great Society program expanded on the New Deal by creating many new federal agencies and domestic policy initiatives that addressed, among other things, poverty reduction, civil rights, education, medical care, social problems in both rural and urban America, and transportation. Major legislation passed under Johnson's direction during this period included the Civil Rights Act of 1964 and the Voting Rights Act of 1965, as well as the creation of Medicare and Medicaid, the Department of Housing and Urban Development, the Department of Transportation, the National Endowment of the Arts, the National Endowment of the Humanities, Head Start, public broadcasting, and numerous initiatives dealing with consumer protection and the environment.

Johnson knew which members of Congress to approach on various issues, as well as the proper timing. He would wait to send bills to Congress until the moment seemed right for maximum support and minimal opposition. Johnson also took care to consult with influential members of Congress and gave them briefings about upcoming bills and appointments. Cabinet members were also responsible for legislation in their policy areas, and when crucial votes were approaching, Johnson would make intense personal appeals to important members whose votes sent cues to others. He was effective at building congressional coalitions in support of his program. However, as the United States became more deeply involved in Vietnam and his administration's prosecution of the war became more controversial, Johnson's political clout began to wane. After the Democrats lost 48 seats in the House during the 1966 midterm elections, Johnson was unable to push the rest of his Great Society through Congress.

THE POLITICAL ENVIRONMENT

Both Roosevelt and Johnson found ways to cultivate the political environment and circumstances presented to them upon taking office, each experiencing tremendous legislative success. Not all presidents have the opportunity or the skill set necessary to achieve legislative success. Moreover, the wider political environment (such as which party controls Congress, whether the economy is thriving, and whether global affairs are calm) can either hurt or help a president's prospects for success. For example, if a president is able to create a friendly environment on the Hill, where Congress is not openly hostile and can receive his initiatives with an open mind, then the president is more likely to have legislative success. Upon taking office in 1981, Ronald Reagan quickly took command of conservative congressional majorities, which passed his tax cut, domestic spending reduction, and defense increase proposals. These initiatives sharply altered the course that domestic social and economic policies had been following since the beginning of the New Deal. Many freshman members of the House, who were swept into office on Reagan's coattails, were nicknamed "Reagan's Robots." And while Republicans had won control of the Senate in 1980, but not the House, there was enough support among these new Republican freshmen to build coalitions around key policies during Reagan's first year in office. Ultimately, however, Reagan's dominance over the congressional agenda was short-lived. His congressional critics regrouped in 1982, and as Congress began to look at the increasing deficit, even Republicans' support on the Hill waned. But Reagan's congenial manner and relaxed style helped establish a positive attitude with Congress over his agenda, which remained an important governing tool throughout his administration.

Other presidents have not been able to create as friendly an environment. For example, Kennedy's relations with Congress were extremely difficult. He had no political base since few Democratic members of Congress rode into office on Kennedy's coattails in 1960. Despite having served in Congress for 14 years (in both the House and the Senate) prior to his election, Kennedy did not have a long track record of sponsoring legislation. He often clashed with the more senior leaders within the Democratic Party, many of whom thought he had run for president "out of turn," skipping ahead of other potential Democratic candidates (including Johnson and Senator Hubert Humphrey of Minnesota, against whom Kennedy competed in the 1960 primaries). Despite the fact that Democrats controlled both houses of Congress during his presidency, Kennedy often was forced to compromise with senior members of his party. As a result, Congress rejected Kennedy's most important domestic legislation, especially in the areas of tax cuts and education.

Richard Nixon's working relationship with Congress is an interesting case study. Nixon hated personal efforts to court Congress, and while both houses remained in control by Democrats after Nixon's election in 1968 (the first time in history that a newly elected president and his party did not win at least one house of Congress), he did enjoy modest legislative success early in his administration. As a pragmatic president, Nixon worked with Democrats (often at the expense of conservatives within the Republican Party) to pass legislation that expanded some of Johnson's Great Society welfare programs. In addition, Nixon is credited with creating the Environmental Protection Agency in 1970. However, Nixon's relationship with Congress was damaged when he challenged the Democratic majority by impounding appropriated funds and asserted a sweeping doctrine of executive privilege under which the White House refused to provide information to congressional committees during the Watergate investigation. Nixon resigned from office in August 1974, when impeachment by the Democratic-controlled House of Representatives was imminent.

Democrat Jimmy Carter served in the White House from 1977 to 1981, during which time Congress was controlled by fellow Democrats. But Carter struggled in his relationship with Democratic leadership on Capitol Hill. Carter was hurt most in this regard by his status as an outsider. Following the primary reforms that took effect in 1972, which took power away from party bosses and gave more powers to voters in the selection of the Democratic presidential nominee, Carter was the first president elected without the support of his party leaders. He was a dark-horse candidate who was mostly unknown to his party in 1976, having served as a one-term governor from Georgia. His reputation as a humble and honest politician helped him get elected in the early post-Watergate years, but his outsider status crippled his legislative effectiveness. Democrats, as a party, had lost power with Carter's election, so they sought to recoup that power in Congress at his expense. Carter also did not cultivate loyalty with Congress, choosing instead to try to pressure Congress into supporting his policy initiatives. Critics also asserted he exhibited an attitude toward Congress of moral superiority. Carter did not build coalitions and was also hurt by a Congress that was reform-minded against the imperial presidencies of the Johnson and Nixon years. Ultimately, the Carter years would be viewed as a legislative failure.

More recently, George W. Bush experienced both highs and lows in public approval as well as in his ability to work with Congress. During his first term—and especially after the September 11, 2001, terrorist attacks on America—Bush benefitted from a willingness (at least temporarily) of the Republican-controlled Congress as well as the public to expand the powers of the presidency to prosecute a "War on Terrorism." He also experienced bipartisan success with the No Child Left Behind Act of 2001, which supported standards-based education reform. Bush also passed tax cuts in 2001 and 2003, though without an accompanying reduction in government spending—to the contrary, government spending actually increased due to higher spending on U.S. military operations in Afghanistan and Iraq—both the budget deficit and the national debt soared. And while Bush signed into law a reform of the Medicare prescription drug coverage in 2003, he also failed to gain bipartisan support on immigration reform proposals in 2007 (with both liberal Democrats and conservative Republicans in Congress unwilling to compromise).

Barack Obama's experience with Congress was somewhat similar to Bush, as both enjoyed unified government during a portion of their eight-year tenures. However, Democrats only controlled both houses of Congress during Obama's first two years in office, though the majorities were significant. As a result, in 2010 Obama was able to pass his signature Affordable Care Act (also known as Obamacare), which greatly reformed health care coverage in the United States. The policymaking process, however, was rancorous and divisive, and the final legislation had no bipartisan support in Congress. Obama also faced a significant economic crisis known as the Great Recession when he first took office, and he and fellow Democrats passed major legislation to bail out many financial institutions as well as the Big Three automakers, along with job creation and consumer protection reform. Republicans were unified in opposition to all of these bills, but with Democrats in control of Congress, they were ultimately unable to derail them. In the 2010 midterm elections, however, Republicans, led by the Tea Party Movement (which embraced smaller government and lower taxes), won control of the House of Representatives. Republicans also won back control of the Senate in 2014, leaving Obama with few options to pass significant legislation. Instead, he turned to using executive orders to advance policy goals, as many other presidents had done before him when faced with divided government. Recent presidents have relied on executive orders, directives issued by the president to manage operations of the federal government, to bypass Congress and enact certain policy changes. In early 2014, Obama stated that "I've got a pen, and I've got a phone," his message to a deadlocked Congress that he would bypass them through executive orders and "calling people together" to get things done in Washington. Most notably, he attempted this with immigration reform and the creation of the Deferred Action for Childhood Arrivals (DACA) program, which grants temporary legal status to children who were brought to the United States illegally.

Donald Trump's relationship with Congress has been complicated at best since he took the oath of office in January 2017. While he has enjoyed legislative success in the areas of tax cuts and repealing government regulations—priorities also shared by his fellow Republicans, who controlled Congress for the first two years of his presidency—he has often been at odds with members of his own party on issues such as trade and health care reform. Many of the policy changes during the early part of Trump's presidency came through signing executive orders (such as

enacting a travel ban against certain countries in an attempt to stop suspected terrorists from entering the United States) or rescinding previous
executive orders by Obama (including withdrawing the United States from
the Trans-Pacific Partnership, considered Obama's signature trade deal).
Democrats won back control of the House of Representatives in the 2018
midterm elections, and in 2019, Trump was impeached in the House for
abuse of power and obstruction of Congress related to his temporary withholding of military aide to Ukraine. Trump was acquitted on both articles
of impeachment in the Republican-controlled Senate in February 2020.

CONCLUSION

While the president has specific constitutional duties related to the legislative process, that role is limited. Whether or not a president can achieve
legislative success in his dealings with Congress can rest on numerous factors and circumstances, political and otherwise. Dealing with a Congress
controlled by members of the president's own party can certainly aid a
president in passing key legislation; party support in Congress is never
guaranteed in every area of governance. Sometimes, political skill can help
a president work with members of Congress when one or both houses are
controlled by the opposing party, which was the case for both Reagan and
Clinton. A president's knowledge of Congress as an institution can also be
beneficial, as Johnson showed in passing major elements of his Great Society agenda. The president's success in achieving his legislative agenda is also
influenced by circumstances, events, and individuals outside the legislative process, such as a strong economy (which can contribute to higher
approval ratings and more money in the federal budget to create new programs) or a large electoral victory that can, if only for a brief time, serve as
a mandate for a presidential agenda.

Ultimately, the president's role in the legislative process speaks directly
to the many challenges of the modern presidency. Presidents are limited in
their constitutional powers to enact policy changes on their own, yet the
American public looks to the president to get things done. Increased public expectations do not always match the constitutional realities of coequal
branches of government. And while a president's approval rating may
experience highs and lows, most modern presidents still remain more popular at their lowest ratings than does Congress with the American public
(approval ratings for Congress have regularly registered under 30%, and as
low as 10%, during the last two decades). As a result, managing a relationship with Congress in pursuit of various legislative policies and agendas
remains a top priority for presidents.

5

The President and the Judicial Branch

Within the system of separation of powers and checks and balances designed by the framers of the U.S. Constitution, the legislative branch makes the law, the executive branch enforces the law, and the judicial branch interprets the law. The federal judiciary maintains its independence to interpret the Constitution and the laws built on the foundation of that document through the fact that justices on the U.S. Supreme Court, as well as all judges on federal district and appeals courts, serve for life terms (provided they behave in accordance with the law). However, the interactions between the courts and the president can be straightforward when dealing with constitutional responsibilities yet complex when factoring in the political environment in which the president is attempting to govern.

The complexity of the relationship is perhaps most apparent when a vacancy occurs on the Supreme Court due to the retirement or death of a sitting member. When that happens, a president gets to nominate his choice for the highest court in the land, pending approval by the Senate. This is perhaps one of the most consequential decisions made during a presidency for a justice can serve for years or even decades, long after the president who selected him or her has left office. The same is true of lower court nominations, so reshaping the judicial branch can go a long way in solidifying a president's policy or ideological legacy. Nominations are not the only way that presidents interact with the judicial branch, however. One of the judicial branch's responsibilities is to ensure that the executive branch conducts itself in accordance with the Constitution. This chapter considers both the constitutional and political consequences of judicial nominations, as well as the impact that Supreme Court decisions can have on presidential powers.

NOMINATIONS TO THE U.S. SUPREME COURT

As outlined in Article II, Section 2, of the Constitution, the president "shall nominate, and by and with the advice and consent of the Senate, shall appoint . . . judges of the Supreme Court." In addition, Article III, Section I, states that "judges, both of the supreme and inferior courts, shall hold their offices during good behavior." Congress holds the power to set the size of the Supreme Court. With passage of the Judiciary Act of 1789, the initial Supreme Court consisted of six justices—a chief justice and five associate justices. The number of justices expanded to 10 in 1863 but was reduced to nine with passage of the Judiciary Act of 1869—a chief justice and eight associate justices.

The size of the Court has not changed since, although Democratic President Franklin D. Roosevelt attempted to "pack the court" following his reelection in 1936. Roosevelt's scheme, which would have increased the size of the Court from nine to 15 justices, stemmed from deep frustration with several Court decisions striking down laws and programs crafted by his administration to combat the Great Depression. When Roosevelt took office in 1933, he had the support of Congress and a majority of the public for his so-called New Deal programs to revive the economy. The Supreme Court, however, did not agree with the president's plans, many of which required a dramatic expansion in the size and scope of the federal government. Seven of the nine justices had been appointed by previous Republican presidents, and the Court regularly struck down major provisions of New Deal legislation beginning in 1935. Frustrated by the lack of vacancies on the Court (no justices retired or passed away during his first term) and determined to capitalize on his huge reelection victory in November 1936, Roosevelt introduced his "court packing" plan in early 1937. At that time, six of the nine justices were over the age of 70, yet none seemed ready to retire. Roosevelt decided that he should be able to make one new nomination to the Court for each of those six justices. This proposal would allow him to "pack the court" with six new justices of his choice, bringing the total number of justices to 15. Despite having a Democratic majority in both the Senate and House of Representatives, Roosevelt was unable to convince Congress to pass the legislation to reorganize the federal judiciary.

However, the mere threat of expanding the size of the Court appeared to spark a change in the Court's attitude toward Roosevelt's New Deal initiatives. Just a few weeks after Roosevelt announced his plan, the Court handed down the first of three 5-4 decisions to uphold New Deal legislation. This move by the Court has come to be known as the famous "switch in time that saved nine." Roosevelt also received his first opportunity to replace a retiring justice in the summer of 1937, the first of a total of nine vacancies on the Court during his 12-plus years in office.

This episode highlights one of the most important structural features—as well as one of the biggest frustrations for presidents—in dealing with the Supreme Court. All justices, along with all other federal judges, are appointed to life terms. While justices and federal judges can be impeached by a majority vote in the House of Representatives and removed by a two-thirds majority vote in the Senate, no Supreme Court justice has ever been removed from office for committing an "impeachable" offense; all have served until retirement or death. The definition of an impeachable offense is not clear, although most would agree that removal should be for a criminal offense or ethical lapse and not purely for partisan or political reasons. In 1805, Justice Samuel Chase, who had been appointed by George Washington, was impeached (but not removed from the bench) due to political opposition to his legal decisions. In the late 1950s and throughout the 1960s, several conservative groups, including the John Birch Society, advocated for the impeachment of Chief Justice Earl Warren, a Dwight Eisenhower appointee, in response to what they considered to be activist and liberal Court rulings (including the landmark decision in *Brown v. Board of Education of Topeka* in 1954, which outlawed segregation in American public schools).

Two unsuccessful impeachment attempts were also brought against Justice William O. Douglas (a Roosevelt appointee) in the House of Representatives. The first attempt came in 1953 after Douglas granted a temporary stay of execution to Julius and Ethel Rosenberg, an American couple convicted of selling atomic bomb secrets to the Russians. The second failed attempt came in 1970 and was led by House Minority Leader Gerald Ford (R-MI) over alleged ethical concerns stemming from Douglas' publications and involvement with a private foundation. In a speech on the House floor, Ford famously stated that an "impeachable offense is whatever a majority of the House of Representatives considers to be at a given moment in history." Yet, despite Ford's definition, attempts to impeach any federal judge, let alone a Supreme Court justice, have been rare.

Given that Supreme Court justices serve for life, each justice has the potential to serve for several decades. Through 2020, a total of 114 men and women have served on the Court, and a total of 17 men have served as chief justice, with an average tenure on the bench of approximately 15 years. However, during the twentieth century, two justices served for particularly notable spans of time. Hugo Black, appointed by Roosevelt in 1937, served for 34 years and one month prior to his retirement in 1971. Similarly, Douglas, also appointed by Roosevelt (in 1939), had served a total of 36 years and six months when he retired in November 1975. Douglas had surpassed the previous longevity record of Stephen J. Field, who had served for 34 years and six months from 1863 (when he was appointed by Abraham Lincoln) to 1897. Ironically, Douglas's replacement on the Court was named by Gerald Ford, who had led the impeachment proceedings against Douglas in the House five years earlier. Ford's selection, John Paul Stevens, also ranked high on the list of longest-serving justices, beginning his 34th year on the Court at the start of the 2009–2010 Supreme Court term and ending the term with his retirement.

When a vacancy occurs on the Court, a potential justice is nominated by the president. Since federal judges are the only public officials to enjoy a lifetime appointment, the nomination and confirmation of a Supreme Court justice represents a significant event during a president's time in office. Quite naturally, every president hopes that the nominee or nominees that he selects will reflect his own political philosophy and policy agenda for years or decades to come. However, there is no guarantee that the confirmation process will go smoothly or that the Senate will approve of the president's choice. The White House must be strategic in its selection of Supreme Court nominees, taking into account the political environment of the period in question, in order to maximize the nominee's chances of gaining Senate confirmation. In addition, it is important to remember that not all nominations are equal. Some nominations, such as the ones to place a new chief justice or replace a conservative justice with a liberal one (or vice versa), can be enormously consequential.

Most presidents, with the help of White House staff, maintain a "short list" of potential nominees ready for when a vacancy should occur. Often, an initial list of judicial nominees takes shape during the transition period after a president wins election in November and prior to the inauguration in January. However, Donald Trump announced his list of potential justices in May 2016, shortly after wrapping up the Republican nomination contest, to reassure conservatives within his party that he would nominate judges with a strict constructionist (which means a literal interpretation) view of the Constitution. Both of his nominations to the Court during his first term in office (Neil Gorsuch in 2017 and Brett Kavanaugh in 2018) had been included on that list.

Presidents rely on many factors in making their decision about whom to nominate, including objective qualifications, policy preferences, political and personal rewards, and building political support. Obviously, a president wants a nomination that will reflect his policy preferences and please his political supporters. The president's political circumstances also affect the confirmation process, including his political strength in the Senate, which votes on his nomination; his level of public approval, which can influence whether the Senate feels political pressure to confirm the nominee; responses of powerful interest groups to potential nominees; and the importance of the nomination (will it fill the position of chief justice or perhaps replace a woman or minority on the Court?). Despite attempts to keep the Court an unbiased and independent institution, presidential appointments are nonetheless political in nature. Several qualified individuals to both the Supreme Court and lower federal courts have been passed over for appointment or failed to be confirmed due to political considerations. The political climate often plays a larger role than merit in who is selected, as do race, gender, religion, and geography.

Nominees to the Supreme Court are always lawyers, although this is not a constitutional requirement, and most have attended top law schools. In recent years, nearly all the justices have been graduates of Harvard, Yale, or Stanford. Previous jobs usually include appellate judgeships (state or federal), jobs within the Justice Department or other parts of the executive branch, or elected office. Most nominees are older than 50, and a majority are from upper or upper middle-class families. Diversity has not been a prominent feature on the Court, although race, ethnicity, and gender have played a more apparent role in selecting nominees since the 1980s. Still, only four women have ever served on the Court—Sandra Day O'Connor (a Reagan nominee who served from 1981 until 2006), Ruth Bader Ginsburg (nominated by Bill Clinton in 1993), and Sonia Sotomayor and Elena Kagan (both nominated by Barack Obama in 2009 and 2010, respectively). Only two African Americans have served on the Court—Thurgood Marshall (nominated by Lyndon Johnson in 1967) and Clarence Thomas (nominated by George H.W. Bush in 1991). In 1986, Reagan appointee Antonin Scalia became the first justice of Italian descent (Samuel Alito, nominated by George W. Bush in 2006, is of Italian descent as well), and Sotomayor is also the first justice of Hispanic descent. Most members of the Court in recent years have been former federal appellate court judges. (Kagan is a recent exception; she had never served as a judge, but she was associate White House Counsel in the Clinton administration, dean of Harvard Law School, and solicitor general in the Obama administration.)

Once the president makes a nomination, the Senate judiciary committee considers it. If the committee approves, the nomination then goes to the entire Senate. The candidate is confirmed if his or her nomination receives support by a simple majority of voters in the Senate. Since 1790, a total of 163 nominations have been made to the Supreme Court. Of these, only 12 have been rejected by the Senate. The three most recent Senate rejections included two of Richard Nixon's nominees (G. Harrold Carswell and Clement Haynsworth) and one Reagan nominee (Robert Bork). One of the closest votes ever to occur in the Senate came in 1991, when Clarence Thomas was only confirmed by a vote of 52–48 following sexual harassment allegations made against him during his confirmation process. The nomination of Brett Kavanaugh in 2018 was also controversial due to allegations of sexual harassment as well as sexual assault, but he was eventually confirmed by a 50–48 vote in the Senate. In addition, the Senate has taken no action on six nominations and postponed a vote on three nominations. Seven individuals have declined the nomination (though no one has done so since 1882), and eight nominations have been withdrawn. Such withdrawals are usually due to impending rejection of the nominee in the Senate confirmation vote or negative public reaction to the nominee.

Senators are not the only political actors involved in the confirmation process. Since 1956, Supreme Court nominees have been closely scrutinized by the American Bar Association (ABA), which rates nominees as "well qualified," "qualified," or "not qualified" (the ABA also rates nominees to district and appellate courts). The ABA has never given a "not qualified" rating for a Supreme Court nominee, but a less-than-unanimous vote among the committee members for a qualified rating can cause a public stir during the confirmation hearings and weaken the nominee's chances. Reagan's nomination of Bork in 1987 and Bush's nomination of Thomas in 1991 both failed to receive unanimous votes from the ABA committee.

Many conservative lawmakers and political observers have denounced the ABA, however, for having a liberal bias in both the policy positions it takes and the ratings it gives judicial nominees. As a result, many Republicans now give less credence to ABA judicial ratings. In 2001, the George W. Bush administration announced that it would not submit the names of judicial nominees to the ABA, eliminating its official role in the nomination process. However, the ABA continued to assess nominees and send its reports to the Senate Judiciary Committee during the Bush years; both chief justice nominee John Roberts and Alito in 2005 received "well qualified" ratings. In 2009, the Obama administration reinstated the practice of submitting the names of judicial nominees to the ABA. Both of Obama's Supreme Court nominees, Sotomayor and Kagan, received "well qualified" ratings.

Beyond the ABA, legal scholars and prominent attorneys also weigh in on a nominee's qualifications. In addition, interest groups can influence the president's selection process, as groups publicly and privately fight for or against nominations. Given the campaign environment once a nomination is announced, it is not surprising that the news media also play a prominent role in the confirmation process. News coverage of Supreme Court nominees since the late 1980s, particularly on cable news, has resulted in intense scrutiny of the nominee's qualifications and legal views. The tone and content of the coverage during the confirmation process often takes on the feel of horse-race coverage similar to presidential campaigns, focusing on whether the nominee is up or down in terms of both Senate and public support, as well as the actions of interest groups in support or opposition of the nomination.

Supreme Court nominations used to occur mostly behind closed doors. In most cases, even the president's political opponents in the Senate acknowledged that it was the president's constitutional prerogative to shape the nation's highest court. However, since the late 1960s, confirmations have become a highly politicized process. Nominees face intense questioning from the Senate Judiciary committee, and cable news outlets provide wall-to-wall coverage of the proceedings, which typically attract higher ratings than typical daytime programming. This was the case with Bork's failed confirmation in 1987, as the conservative judge did not shy away from telling Democratic senators exactly how he would rule on cases (such as abortion rights) if such a case came before him on the Court. Since then, most judicial nominees shy away from providing candid answers at their confirmation hearings. Media attention became particularly intense during the confirmation hearings of both Thomas and Kavanaugh due to the sexual misconduct allegations made against each nominee.

PRESIDENTIAL LEGACIES

Historically, presidents have selected a new justice in an average of every two years. Some presidents, however, get fewer opportunities than average. Both Bill Clinton and George W. Bush filled only two Supreme Court openings each during their respective eight years in office. The period between 1994 (when Clinton made his second nomination of Stephen Breyer) and 2005 (when Bush announced his first nomination of John Roberts) was the longest stretch in which there were no vacancies on the Court since the 1820s.

George Washington holds the record for the most appointments, since he appointed the six original justices plus four additional justices before the end of his second term in 1797. During his twelve-plus years as president, Franklin D. Roosevelt came close to Washington's record. He made eight appointments to the Court and elevated Justice Harlan Fiske Stone to chief justice. Not all presidents, however, are happy with their choices to the Court once confirmed. In a much-quoted story, Dwight Eisenhower was asked just before leaving office in 1961 if he had made any mistakes as president. He responded with a yes, explaining that two of his five nominees to the Supreme Court—Chief Justice Earl Warren and Associate Justice William Brennan—had proven to be much more liberal than Eisenhower had anticipated.

Presidents try to nominate an individual to satisfy their own agenda. For example, Ronald Reagan promised voters to nominate the first woman to the Court during the 1980 presidential campaign and kept that promise by nominating Sandra Day O'Connor in 1981. But even such an historic appointment was not without some controversy. First, with so few women holding judicial appointments at the time, and even fewer with a conservative background, Reagan did not have a long list of potential women candidates to consider. He eventually looked outside of the federal court system to find his nominee; O'Connor was a member of the Arizona State Court of Appeals at the time. Second, upon O'Connor's nomination, Reagan was criticized by both liberals and conservatives for his choice. Liberals were happy to see the first woman join the high court, but they feared that O'Connor's positions, particularly on women's issues, would be too conservative. Conservatives, on the other hand, feared that O'Connor lacked adequate federal judicial experience and knowledge of the U.S. Constitution and that she would also uphold abortion rights (Reagan had campaigned to make abortion illegal). Nearly 25 years later, when she announced her retirement from the Court in 2005, O'Connor had earned a reputation as a pragmatic and often centrist swing vote on issues such as abortion, affirmative action, and privacy rights, taking positions that at times were out of step with Reagan's more conservative policy agenda.

Chief Justice William Rehnquist left a strong legacy for two presidents. First nominated as an associate justice by Richard Nixon in 1971 and confirmed in early 1972, Rehnquist was a strong advocate for the law-and-order, states' rights approach to the U.S. Constitution that Nixon advocated. Within three years of Rehnquist's confirmation to the Court, Nixon had resigned from office in 1974 because of the Watergate scandal. In 1986, Rehnquist was elevated to the position of Chief Justice by Reagan. Prior to his death in 2005, more than 33 years after his initial nomination—and 31 years following Nixon's resignation—Rehnquist was closing in on the record as the Court's longest-serving member. Nixon had chosen well for the purposes of a long-lasting political legacy, as did Reagan with his elevation of Rehnquist to Chief Justice.

NOMINATIONS TO DISTRICT AND APPELLATE COURTS

The U.S. Constitution provides little guidance on development of the federal court system. Article III states that a supreme court will exist and that other federal courts would be established by Congress as needed. From the time Congress passed the Judiciary Act of 1789 establishing the first lower federal courts, Congress has continued to expand the size of the federal judiciary in order to accommodate the nation's growing size (in terms of both land area and population) and complexity (in terms of public administration and law).

Today, more than 100 courts make up the federal judicial branch. The lowest federal courts are the district courts, which serve as trial courts with juries. If a district court case is appealed, the next step is a federal court of appeals. There are 12 federal judicial circuits (or territories), and each has its own court of appeals. Congress has also created other specialty courts over the years: the U.S. Court of Military Appeals, which hears appeals of military courts-martial; the U.S. Court of Federal Claims, where cases in which the U.S. government has been sued for damages are tried; and the U.S. Court of International Trade, which hears cases involving appeals to rulings by the U.S. Customs Office.

Just as with the Supreme Court, district and appeals court judges serve lifetime terms. When a vacancy occurs, the president nominates individuals who then must be confirmed by a majority vote in the Senate; federal judges can also be removed from the bench through impeachment in the House of Representatives and removal by a trial in the Senate. A total of 13 federal judges have been impeached in U.S. history, including Supreme Court Justice Samuel Chase, who was impeached in 1804 but escaped conviction by the Senate. Seven of those federal judges were eventually convicted in the Senate and removed from office.

Given the number of federal judgeships and the fact that they are lifetime appointments, presidents can have significant influence over the makeup of the judicial branch by nominating judges who are sympathetic to their policy agendas. While presidents may not get the opportunity to nominate individuals to the Supreme Court often, they do make more frequent selections for lower court judgeships (about 200 per four-year term). While lower court appointments are not as high profile as those to the Supreme Court, they are still important decisions made by the White House with the potential for a long-lasting effect on the policy agenda.

Judicial selections are influenced by both policy and partisan considerations. For example, the Reagan administration viewed the federal courts to be too activist in pursuing a liberal policy agenda, and so it sought to counterbalance that alleged flaw by seating as many conservative judges as possible. This goal can have partisan appeal as well; Donald Trump has frequently reminded social conservatives who might dislike him for personal reasons that he has placed many conservative judges on the federal bench.

There are currently more than 850 federal judgeships throughout the lower courts of the judicial branch, with the number of district and appellate judges more than doubling since 1950. This number often fluctuates, as Congress either increases or decreases the number of judicial positions (the latter rarely occurs) or as vacancies open up due to the retirement or death of sitting judges. Some presidents have greatly benefitted from the addition of several lower court judgeships while in office, as having more vacancies provides a greater opportunity to reshape the federal bench to reflect the president's governing philosophy. The Constitution set forth no specific requirements for qualifications for these positions. However, legal qualifications for the position (such as holding a law degree or having meaningful professional experience in the legal field) and being sympathetic to the president's political views are generally acknowledged to be important factors for potential nominees in the selection process.

Due to the volume of appointments, the president does not usually play a direct role in nominating individuals to lower court positions. The Department of Justice, usually through the deputy attorney general, helps to screen potential nominees. Other White House staff members assist in the screening process as well. For these appointments, members of Congress also typically recommend potential nominees.

Members of the U.S. Senate have traditionally relied on what is known as senatorial courtesy in the selection and nomination process, most notably for district court nominations. This tradition involving federal appointments dates back to the early days of the republic. With the practice of senatorial courtesy, senators from the state where a vacancy has occurred are given the opportunity to have a say in the president's nomination. This is accomplished through the so-called blue slip procedure, in which senators from the home state of the judicial nominee receive notification of the nomination by letter from the chair of the Senate Judiciary Committee. Along with the notice, the senator receives a blue sheet of paper on which he or she can comment on the nominee. If the senator does not return the blue slip, it is understood to mean that the senator does not approve of the nomination, and it does not go forward for Senate consideration. In addition, if the senator is not consulted, then he or she has the right to request that the confirmation be denied. For many years, senators holding blue slips had virtual one-person veto power to block a nomination. Knowing this, presidents usually had to heed the views of those senators when seeking to fill lower court vacancies.

Over the last two or three decades, however, notions of "senatorial courtesy" and the practice of blue-slipping have eroded significantly, to the point that both appear to be relics of a bygone era of Senate collegiality. Depending on who is chairing the Senate Judiciary Committee, there have been times when only those senators from the president's party have been allowed to use the practice of senatorial courtesy. For example, during the last six years of the Clinton administration, when Republicans controlled the Senate, Judiciary Committee Chairman Orrin Hatch (R-UT) allowed Republican senators to veto Clinton nominees through the blue-slip procedure. But when fellow Republican George W. Bush entered the White House in 2001, Hatch attempted to weaken the blue-slip procedure to deny home-state Democrats the same opportunity. In 2019, the blue-slip procedure was completely ignored by the Senate's Republican leaders. They engineered the confirmation of several Trump nominees without first securing the support of their (Democratic) home-state senators.

The increased emphasis by presidents in recent years to shape the federal court system to better match their policy agendas and political philosophies has also increased the contentiousness over nominations in the Senate confirmation process. This was a significant issue during the George W. Bush presidency, as Senate Democrats attempted to block several of Bush's judicial appointments, especially at the appellate court level. Prior to 2001, senators had rarely relied on the filibuster to derail a judicial nomination. (A filibuster is often used by the minority party in the Senate to kill legislation; a filibuster represents unlimited Senate debate, which can be used by the minority party to slow the progress of a bill to the point that passage becomes impossible. To end a filibuster, a vote of cloture must be taken, which requires 60 votes for success.) But when Bush first became president, Democrats in the Senate used the filibuster to successfully block several of his judicial nominations to lower federal courts that they believed were too extreme in their conservative views.

Democrats successfully blocked several of Bush's nominees during his first four years in office, despite the fact that they were the minority party in the Senate. Senate Republicans became so frustrated that they threatened to use the "nuclear option" to bypass the opposition by Democrats. This nuclear option was a proposal to change the Senate rules to allow a vote of cloture with only a simple majority of votes (51) as opposed to 60, thereby taking away the Democrats' power to block a judicial nominee. In 2005, a bipartisan compromise brokered by 14 senators from both parties (nicknamed the "Gang of 14") resulted in an agreement by Democrats to stop filibusters of Bush's judicial nominees except in "extraordinary circumstances." However, during Obama's presidency, Republicans used filibusters to block several of his judicial nominees. But at this point Democrats controlled the Senate, and Majority Leader Harry Reid (NV) and fellow Democrats responded to what they described as GOP obstruction by voting in favor of the "nuclear option." This changed filibuster rules on all confirmations except those to the Supreme Court.

After Donald Trump's election in 2016, some Democrats (though not Reid) stated they regretted eliminating the filibuster for judicial nominations. This position stemmed from the fact that during the first three years of Trump's presidency, Republicans controlled the Senate. For all practical purposes, this meant that Republicans, who held 53 seats in the Senate, did not need any Democratic support at all to reach the 51 votes necessary to confirm any Trump Cabinet or judicial nomination. In 2017, the Republican-led Senate also eliminated the filibuster for Supreme Court nominations, enabling them to confirm both Neil Gorsuch and Brett Kavanaugh despite near-unanimous opposition from Democrats.

PRESIDENTIAL INTERACTIONS WITH THE JUDICIAL BRANCH

As Alexander Hamilton explained in *Federalist* 78, the Supreme Court "has neither force nor will, but merely judgment." The cooperation of many other political actors at the federal, state, and local levels is necessary to successfully implement decisions by the Court. Chief among those actors is the president, who, along with the rest of the executive branch, is responsible for the implementation of federal laws.

Perhaps the most important position within the executive branch regarding the Supreme Court and its operations is the U.S. Solicitor General. As the third-ranking official in the Department of Justice, behind the Attorney General and the Deputy Attorney General, the Solicitor General holds one of the most important legal positions within government. It is also the only high-level position within the federal government that requires, through statute, that the person holding the position be "learned in the law." The solicitor general is nominated by the president and confirmed by the Senate. Created in 1870, the Office of Solicitor General generally includes 25–30 attorneys and administrative support. The office is responsible for directly arguing cases before the Court when the federal government is a party to a case. In addition, the solicitor general decides which cases among those lost by the federal government should be appealed to a higher federal court. This responsibility makes it the gatekeeper for all appellate litigation involving the federal government. In an indication of the significance that the solicitor general can have in the selection of cases or their outcomes, the position is often referred to as the 10th Supreme Court justice.

While decisions by the Court ultimately affect all Americans, public officials who are called upon to immediately respond to Court rulings include the solicitor general, the attorney general, cabinet heads, and legal counsel for executive branch agencies. Since decisions handed down by the Court are not self-executing, these executive branch officials play an important role in interpreting judicial rulings and advising the president and others within the executive branch on how to implement its decisions. State attorney generals play a similar role in advising state and local officials on implementation strategies of Supreme Court decisions. Often, the Court is at the mercy of these other political actors to make sure that the ruling goes into effect. The struggle to implement the *Brown v. Board of Education of Topeka* (1954) that ended segregation in public schools provides an important example. In the aftermath of that decision, many Southern states and cities defiantly refused to desegregate their schools. In 1957, Dwight Eisenhower actually sent National Guard troops into Little Rock, Arkansas, to end racial segregation at the city's all-white Little Rock Central High and to quell the violence over the federally mandated enrollment of nine African American students. John F. Kennedy took similar action in 1962 to force integration at the University of Mississippi to allow enrollment by James Meredith, the first African American student to attend "Ole Miss."

Presidents have also ignored rulings by the Supreme Court, blocked attempts at their implementation, or attempted to strike back at the Court for decisions of which the president disapproved. Since the earliest days of the republic, presidents have at times found themselves frustrated by the Supreme Court's power of judicial review. Considered the cornerstone of American constitutional law, judicial review denotes the power of a court to review a policy of government and to invalidate that policy if it is contrary to constitutional principles. The Constitution remains silent on the issue of judicial review (the framers did not discuss this legal concept at the Constitutional Convention, though many assumed something similar in giving courts the power to interpret the laws), though the Supreme Court assumed the power to review legislation as early as 1796, when it upheld a federal tax on carriages as valid.

The main power of judicial review comes from the Court's ability to strike down legislation, which occurred for the first time in U.S. history in *Marbury v. Madison* (1803). The case stemmed from the 1800 elections, in which the Federalists and John Adams lost the presidency and both houses of Congress to the Jeffersonian Republicans. Adams and the Federalists decided to try to preserve their influence over the national government through the courts. In the days following the election—but before the Jeffersonian Republicans took over in Washington—Federalists in Congress passed the Judiciary Act of 1801. This law created several additional federal judgeships for Adams to fill before leaving office. William Marbury was a Federalist politician appointed by Adams to fill a new position as a justice of the peace for the District of Columbia. The Senate confirmed Marbury's commission on March 3, 1801, Adams' last day in office. John Marshall, who was then Secretary of State, placed the seal of the United States on the letter of commission, which was ready to be delivered to Marbury. Marshall's brother James was to deliver the commission, but it went undelivered and was eventually lost. Thomas Jefferson became president the next day. He ordered his new Secretary of State, James Madison, to not deliver copies of the commission to Marbury and other Federalists. As a result, they failed to get their judgeships. Jefferson then mounted an effort to repeal the Judiciary Act of 1801. Congress, now controlled by Jeffersonian Republicans, obliged and even abolished the Supreme Court term of 1802.

The following year, Marbury filed suit against Madison in the Supreme Court. He asked the Court, under its original jurisdiction, to issue a writ of mandamus—an order directing Madison to deliver the disputed judicial commission to Marbury. By then, Marshall was the new Chief Justice. In fact, he had been appointed by Adams and confirmed by the Federalist-controlled Congress in the last weeks of his administration. But despite this clear conflict of interest, he did not recuse himself from the case. The Court ruled that Marbury had a legal right to his commission and that the Jefferson administration was wrong to deny him. However, the Court did not issue the writ of mandamus because it indicated that it had no legal authority to do so. The Court's presumed authority to issue the writ was based on Section 13 of the Judiciary Act of 1789, which granted the Court authority to issue writs of mandamus "in cases warranted by the principles and usages of law." But in Marshall's opinion, the Court could not do that since the relevant provision of Section 13 expanded the Court's original jurisdiction in an unconstitutional manner. Article III, Section 2, expressly provides that Congress has the authority to regulate the appellate jurisdiction of the Court, which also implies that Congress has no such authority to regulate or change original jurisdiction. Therefore, Section 13 was invalid as it permitted the Court to issue a writ of mandamus in a case under the Court's original jurisdiction. This was the first time that the Court held an act of Congress to be null and void.

Beyond the legendary dispute between Jefferson and Marshall, President Andrew Jackson also challenged the authority of the Supreme Court's power of judicial review. When Congress passed a bill in 1832 to recharter the Second Bank of the United States, Jackson vetoed the bill. He declared in his lengthy veto message that the Supreme Court alone did not have the power to determine the constitutionality of laws. Jackson wrote: "The Congress, the Executive, and the Court must each for itself be guided by its own opinion of the Constitution. Each public officer who takes an oath to support the Constitution swears that he will support it as he understands it, and not as it is understood by others. It is as much the duty of the House of Representatives, of the Senate, and of the President to decide upon the constitutionality of any bill or resolution which may be presented to them for passage or approval as it is of the supreme judges when it may be brought before them for judicial decision." This was just one of several occasions in which Jackson challenged the rulings of Chief Justice Marshall and the Court. In 1832, for example, Jackson allegedly declared, "Well, John Marshall has made his decision, now let him enforce it," after the Court ruled to protect Indian tribal sovereignty against encroachment by state laws.

INTERPRETING PRESIDENTIAL POWERS

The Court also makes decisions that define the parameters of presidential powers. The Constitution provides few enumerated powers to the office of the presidency, but the expansion of the executive branch's implied or inherent powers has often, though not always, come through Supreme Court decisions. One of the most often cited examples of a Supreme Court ruling that expanded presidential power is *U.S. v. Curtiss-Wright Export Corp.* (1936). Franklin D. Roosevelt had placed an arms embargo on countries at war in South America, and the Curtiss-Wright Export Corporation was indicted for ignoring the embargo. The Court ruled that the embargo was constitutional and that the president could be empowered to act alone involving foreign affairs.

This ruling established an important precedent in the expansion of presidential powers in the realm of foreign affairs. Other notable expansions of presidential powers include *The Prize Cases* (1863), in which the Court ruled that Abraham Lincoln's blockade of southern ports during the Civil War was indeed constitutional, even though it was considered an act of war against the Confederate Army. Also, in one of the Court's most infamous rulings in 1944 (*Korematsu v. United States*), it declared constitutional Roosevelt's decision to relocate and place Japanese Americans in internment camps during World War II.

However, the Court has also issued rulings restricting presidential powers or handed down decisions that rule against a particular president's actions yet expand presidential authority. The latter occurred in two prominent decisions. In 1952, the Court both restricted and expanded presidential powers in *Youngstown Sheet and Tube Co. v. Sawyer*. Harry Truman wanted to seize the nation's steel mills to prevent a strike, which he felt would hurt the U.S. military during a time when it was deeply engaged in the Korean War. He subsequently issued an executive order to have the Secretary of Commerce seize and operate the mills in accordance with American military needs. Truman argued that as commander in chief, he had constitutional authority to take this action. Back in 1947, however, Congress had explicitly voted down a provision in the Tart-Hartley Act (which limited strikes by labor unions) that would have given the president the type of power that Truman was claiming. In its 1952 decision, the Court ruled that the president could not take control of the U.S. steel industry without the approval of Congress. Yet, the Court also recognized in its ruling that the president does have certain inherent powers to take actions not specified by the Constitution.

Similarly, in *U.S. v. Nixon* (1974), Richard Nixon challenged the special prosecutor's subpoena for White House tapes during the Watergate investigation. While the Court ruled against Nixon and made him turn over the tapes (which implicated him in the cover-up of the Watergate scandal and led to his resignation from office), the Court also claimed for the first time that "executive privilege" does exist (which means that a president can have private conversations with advisors). However, the Court did not support unlimited executive privilege, which Nixon had sought.

More recently, the Court ruled unanimously in *NLRB v. Noel Canning* (2014) that the president cannot use his authority under the Constitution's Recess Appointment Clause to appoint public officials unless the Senate is in recess and thus cannot conduct Senate business. The ruling invalidated four appointments by Barack Obama—three to the National Labor Relations Board and the other the director of the Consumer Financial Protection Bureau—during what the White House considered to be a recess. However, the Court ruled that despite a break in the Senate's work every three days in short pro forma sessions (in which no business was conducted), that could not be considered a recess, and thus the appointments were unconstitutional.

CONCLUSION

Like Congress, the federal judiciary, especially the Supreme Court, has many opportunities to place constitutional checks on presidential authority and actions. The life tenure of federal judges, combined with the fact that Supreme Court decisions can only be overturned through a constitutional amendment or later Court decisions, has at times posed a significant challenge to presidents seeking to advance their policy agendas. But while presidents have no control over the Supreme Court's power to interpret the constitutionality of federal laws and actions by federal officials, the president does play a significant role in the selection of Supreme Court justices and federal judges. In addition, presidents can use the office of the U.S. solicitor general to influence the docket of cases pending in federal courts, including the Supreme Court. Presidents have been both enabled and restrained in expanding presidential powers, and some presidents have also had success in reshaping parts of the federal judiciary to reflect their ideological perspective and political agenda. Ultimately, the relationship between the president and the federal judiciary represents the challenging task of each trying to balance their constitutional functions against the backdrop of the current political environment.

6

The President and the Executive Branch

The job of president includes many roles, both constitutional and ceremonial. In addition to serving as commander in chief of the nation's military, the president is also both head of state and head of government. The former is mostly ceremonial in that presidents, for example, represent the United States on the world stage. The latter refers to the fact that the president is the chief executive of the federal government. What does it mean to be the chief executive? Some compare it to being the chief executive officer of a large corporation. In some respects, the comparison is understandable, even though the jobs are vastly different in size and scope. In American political life, the president is held responsible for the operation of the government, and if the government fails to meet popular expectations, the president takes the blame. The president has many responsibilities in this role, and many factors can affect his performance.

This chapter considers the constitutional and political implications of the president's relationship with the executive branch of government. The federal government employs more than three million people, and nearly all are found within the complicated bureaucratic structure of agencies within the executive branch. Therefore, organization is crucial in understanding how the bureaucracy works and how the president manages the day-to-day operation of the federal government.

The Executive Office of the President (EOP), created in 1939 to help the president manage this responsibility, has evolved into a highly specialized and compartmentalized bureaucracy. The EOP carries out such institutionalized staff functions as program planning and review, budgeting, implementation, and evaluation. Within that structure is the Cabinet and White House staff, who are part of the president's team regarding both policy and political matters. Throughout American history, vice presidents and first ladies have also played an important role in how the president governs.

CHIEF EXECUTIVES AND THE BUREAUCRACY

The president's relationship with the executive branch comes from three distinct clauses in Article II of the Constitution: "'The executive Power shall be vested in a President of the United States of America'; 'He shall nominate, and by and with the Advice and Consent of the Senate, shall appoint Ambassadors, other public Ministers and Consuls, . . . and all other Officers of the United States, whose Appointments are not herein otherwise provided for, and which shall be established by Law: but the Congress may by Law vest the Appointment of such inferior Officers, as they think proper, in the President alone, in the Courts of Law, or in the Heads of Departments'; and, 'He may require the Opinion, in writing, of the principal Officer in each of the executive Departments, upon any subject relating to the Duties of their respective Offices.'" As with other aspects of the Constitution, a few specifics are provided to explicitly outline the president's powers in this role.

During the first 100 years of the nation, the federal bureaucracy that each president oversaw remained small. The first Congress created the first four departments in the Executive Branch: Treasury, State, and War, plus an Attorney General for legal advice. These same departments existed in the government under the Articles of Confederation. The departments contained a few employees apart from the Secretary and minimal staff.

During the first few decades of the nineteenth century, the federal government employed fewer than 10,000 people. By the time Andrew Jackson became president in 1829, however, the "spoils system" of political patronage began to emerge. Jackson's time in office coincided with the beginning of modern political parties. Appointments to government positions were increasingly reserved for those who supported the party and its presidential candidate. This system of patronage continued and deepened until corruption, incompetence, and the assassination of James Garfield in 1881 by Charles Guiteau, who was unable to secure a government job because of the spoils system, finally convinced lawmakers to pass meaningful civil service reform. The Pendleton Civil Service Reform

Act of 1881 applied only to federal employees and made merit the criteria for hiring and firing in all but cabinet-level jobs. By the time Franklin D. Roosevelt took office in 1933, 80 percent of federal workers were included in the merit system.

Today, the more than three million people who work for the federal government have a direct impact on the daily lives of Americans. That number includes all branches of the U.S. military (Army, Navy, Air Force, Marine Corps, and Coast Guard). By definition, a bureaucracy is a system of civil servants and political appointees who implement congressional or presidential decisions. Yet, only a small number of political appointees at the top of various agencies rotate in and out with the election of a new president, leaving most of the remaining employees to serve long careers in government. The paradox of the bureaucracy is that the same organization that accomplishes so many big tasks also does things that are inefficient and wasteful, which is why citizens often take such a dim view of this part of government.

The modern federal bureaucracy includes various departments and agencies that deal with specialized policies and programs. There are 15 cabinet departments (discussed in the following section), as well as independent agencies such as the CIA (Central Intelligence Agency) and NASA (National Aeronautics and Space Administration), that have a narrower scope of responsibilities. The federal government also includes regulatory agencies such as the Environmental Protection Agency (EPA), Federal Communications Commission (FCC), Federal Election Commission (FEC), and Securities and Exchange Commission (SEC) and government corporations that are run like private companies but receive government funding; examples include Amtrak, the U.S. Postal Service, and Fannie Mae and Freddie Mac, which are federal housing finance agencies. Ultimately, the federal bureaucracy holds great power within the government through considerable discretion in day-to-day policy implementation. This independent power can be checked by the other branches of the government: the president can appoint and reorganize areas of the bureaucracy, Congress controls the budget and has oversight, and the courts can ensure that agencies act according to legislative intent. Bureaucratic "drift" can occur, however, when bureaucrats implement policies in a way that favors their own political objectives rather than the original intentions of the legislation.

THE CABINET

There are 15 executive branch departments, which are known collectively as the Cabinet. Each is headed by a secretary (except the Department of Justice, which is led by the Attorney General) who is nominated by the president. Cabinet departments include State (created in 1789), Treasury (1789), Defense (1947; previously War, 1789), Justice (1870; previously the Office of Attorney General, 1789), Interior (1849), Agriculture (1862), Commerce (1903), Labor (1913), Health and Human Services (1953; previously Health, Education, and Welfare), Housing and Urban Development (1965), Transportation (1967), Energy (1977), Education (1979), Veterans Affairs (1988), and Homeland Security (2002). The four largest departments are Defense, Veterans Affairs, Homeland Security, and Justice.

By custom and tradition, the Cabinet officers meet as a group to advise the president on the operations of their departments. Department secretaries must be confirmed by the Senate, and they must testify before congressional committees and secure approval from those committees for department budgets. This is how Congress checks authority within this part of the executive branch. The Cabinet is usually selected for political reasons as opposed to personal ones; considerations of diversity and geography often influence certain selections. Although many Cabinets are filled with distinguished members, rarely do they serve as a collective source of advice for the president. The inner cabinet is considered to include State, Defense, Treasury, and Justice, and the men and women holding these positions are more likely to serve as close advisors to the president. Cabinet rank is typically accorded to the Vice President and the U.S. Representative to the United Nations so they can attend Cabinet meetings. Presidents can grant Cabinet rank and the privileges that go with it to whatever agency director they choose; for example, presidents have awarded Cabinet status to the Director of the Central Intelligence Agency (CIA) and the Director of the Office of Management and Budget (OMB).

EXECUTIVE OFFICE OF THE PRESIDENT

Various units exist within the Executive Office of the President (EOP) and are used by the president to advance White House programs and policies. As with many developments in the modern presidency, the size of the White House staff increased dramatically with Franklin D. Roosevelt's presidency and his many New Deal programs and initiatives. This posed a problem in terms of organization as well as management. To address these problems, Roosevelt created the Committee on Administrative Management, headed by Lewis Brownlow. The Brownlow Committee produced a report with significant institutional recommendations in 1937, famously concluding "the President needs help." The EOP was created in 1939 in direct response. It included the White House Office and the Bureau of the Budget (today known as OMB). Two other important offices were added to the EOP within the decade—the Council of Economic Advisers (created in 1946) and the National Security Council (created in 1947).

WHITE HOUSE STAFF

Most of the president's closest advisors can be found among the White House staff. Many of these people have been rewarded by the president for loyal service long before he ever reached the Oval Office. These are usually men and women who have proven themselves to the president in past election campaigns or as members of their senatorial or gubernatorial staffs. Most presidents now have a chief of staff, whose responsibility it is to manage White House staff and coordinate their activities on behalf of the president. An effective chief of staff serves as the gatekeeper to the president (determining who sees the president, what memos cross his desk, etc.), helps to manage the daily schedule, and keeps the president disciplined and focused on important policy and political issues. Other high-profile White House staff members can include the press secretary, the staff secretary (who is in charge of handling the communication of messages and the circulation of memos and documents between the president and his senior staff), czars (an official chosen to focus on a specific policy area), the White House counsel (the president's top advisor on legal issues), the director of the Office of Personnel Management (who is in charge of seeking out individuals to serve in the administration), and the national security advisor. On average, the EOP includes approximately 500 staff members.

Presidents have differed on how they organize the White House staff. Since the creation of the modern White House during the Franklin D. Roosevelt administration, there have been only four models of organization: competitive, hierarchical, collegial, and modified.

A competitive system is one in which the advisors do not have set roles, reporting to the president based on specific policy assignments. As a management technique, the competitive style is somewhat chaotic and difficult to maintain because it requires excessive presidential participation. Only Roosevelt has used this staffing system, believing that competition among advisors would provide the best policy results. Both Dwight Eisenhower and Richard Nixon employed hierarchical arrangements with strict hierarchical staff arrangements; a chief of staff is key in this scenario as the gatekeeper who controls and coordinates the flow of paper as well as access to the president. Gerald Ford and Jimmy Carter, following Nixon's resignation due to the Watergate scandal, designed their staffing arrangements based on a collegial system with an open-door policy and no hierarchy (meaning that all advisors are equal in the eyes of the president). A modified system (used by Ronald Reagan and other presidents since) sought the best of both worlds—the ability to prioritize and control without a loss of access and spontaneity. They created a modified collegial system and set up a hierarchy for prioritizing coupled with collegiality for widespread access to ideas.

PRESIDENTIAL MANAGEMENT OF THE BUREAUCRACY

The EOP provides the president with managerial capacity over the bureaucracy, including appointments, budgeting, regulatory review, executive orders, and signing statements. The expansion of the federal government with Roosevelt's New Deal greatly increased the size of the civil service work force, and most of the new hires were Democrats. In 1953, when Eisenhower became the first Republican president in 20 years, he was faced with a predominantly Democratic bureaucracy. As a result, he issued an executive order that created nearly 1000 new appointed positions for the specific purpose of adding Republicans to his administration. Prior to this executive order, top-level jobs (those below Secretary and Under Secretary positions) were filled by promoting career civil servants. After Eisenhower's action, career civil servants had to compete with the president's appointments for those positions.

Budgeting is a powerful presidential tool, as the size of the budget determines how much an agency can accomplish. Presidents cannot abolish programs, agencies, or departments, but they can promote programs by adding to their budgets or downgrade programs by not providing needed funds within budget requests to Congress. Similarly, in the regulatory review process, the OMB and other presidential agencies often perform and share analyses of the rules created to implement congressional legislation.

Although Congress tasks the departments and agencies with implementing and administering the legislation they produce, as the chief executive, the president is ultimately responsible for the implementation of legislation. Consequently, the president has considerable leeway in implementing what is at times complicated or vague legislation. An executive order is a presidential directive that tells bureaucrats within the federal government how to interpret the legislation. These orders are typically crafted with the president's agenda, goals, and ideology in mind.

The use of executive orders began with George Washington, and as time passed, other presidents used them to momentous effect. For example, Thomas Jefferson used an executive order to approve the Louisiana Purchase, and Abraham Lincoln's Emancipation Proclamation was an executive order. These examples show just how far-ranging and important executive orders can be. However, the orders are not absolute; they have the force of law, but can be checked by a court ruling or subsequent congressional action.

Although Congress limits the president's ability to enact his agenda by legislation, executive orders provide another avenue for the president to advance some portions of his agenda without encountering the complexities of the legislative process.

Finally, presidents can also rely on signing statements to both implement and interpret legislation as passed by Congress. When a president receives a piece of legislation, he has two options: sign it and make it law or veto it. Since James Monroe, not only have presidents simply signed or not signed the bill, they have also issued commentary on the legislation with their understanding of how the law should be implemented. While they do not have the force of law that executive orders contain, signing statements provide guidance for agencies in their rulemaking and an opportunity to influence future judicial interpretations of the laws in question. Modern presidents, particularly those faced with divided government, have frequently used signing statements to assert the power and prerogatives of the presidency. For example, George W. Bush asserted in 76 distinct signing statements a phrase that encapsulated the president's position, particularly as a "war president" following the 9/11 attacks: "supervise the unitary executive branch." This highlighted the Bush administration's view that presidents have broad and sweeping powers during a time of national emergency or war.

OFFICE OF THE VICE PRESIDENT

The office of vice president enjoys a unique status within the American system of government. The position leaves the occupant a "heartbeat away" from the presidency. Indeed, of the 48 men who have held the position of vice president, 14 went on to become president themselves, with nine succeeding to the position due to presidential death or resignation. Yet, the framers of America's constitution had only a minor interest in the office when they designed the architecture of the government. Alexander Hamilton devoted only two paragraphs to it in *Federalist* 68, and his comments offered no insights or guidance about the primary purposes of the office. Although other documents reflect Anti-Federalist concerns over the vice president's role in the Senate, they reveal nothing about the nature of the office, nor do they shed any light on its theoretical foundations.

The first vice president, John Adams, claimed, "My country has in its wisdom contrived for me the most insignificant office that ever the invention of man contrived or his imagination conceived." More than 150 years later, Franklin D. Roosevelt's first vice president, John Nance Garner, colorfully declared that the office was "hardly worth a pitcher of spit." These disparaging remarks reflected the fact that the position has only two official functions that hardly make for a full day-to-day schedule. In the event of a tie vote in the Senate, the vice president casts the deciding vote. In the event of the death, incapacitation, resignation or impeachment of the president, the vice president assumes the job of president. Thus, there is no constitutionally defined role as to how the vice president should spend his time. The Constitution, as ratified in 1789, mentions the vice presidency four specific times; there are three additional amendments that deal with the position. The four initial references sum up the job description as designed by the framers: "The Vice President of the United States shall be President of the Senate, but shall have no Vote, unless they be equally divided" (Article II, Section 3); "The executive Power shall be vested in a President of the United States of America. He shall hold his Office during the Term of four Years, and, together with the Vice-President chosen for the same Term, be elected, as follows . . ." (Article II, Section 1); "In Case of the Removal of the President from Office, or of his Death, Resignation, or Inability to discharge the Powers and Duties of the said Office, the same shall devolve on the Vice President, and the Congress may by Law provide for the Case of Removal, Death, Resignation or Inability, both of the President and Vice President, declaring what Officer shall then act as President, and such Officer shall act accordingly, until the Disability be removed, or a President shall be elected" (Article II, Section I, modified by the 20th and 25th amendments); "The President, Vice President and all civil Officers of the United States, shall be removed from Office on Impeachment for, and Conviction of, Treason, Bribery, or other high Crimes and Misdemeanors" (Article II, Section 4).

In addition, as per the framers' intentions, the Constitution required electors to vote for two undifferentiated candidates during presidential elections. This system was supposed to produce a president and his presumed successor and, in so doing, preserve stability and the unified and steady progress of the presidency. The framers envisioned vice presidents to be among their presidents' closest advisors, supporting presidential policymaking and getting on-the-job training for the nation's highest office.

Unfortunately, the relationship between the president and vice president did not evolve as the architects of the Constitution hoped it would. Instead, personal incompatibilities soon undermined original intent, relegating the vice presidency to a back seat in executive politics. The Twelfth Amendment (which required each elector to cast distinct votes for president and vice president instead of two votes for president) formally acknowledged the inferiority of the vice presidency and subordinated it to the presidency in a way the framers never intended.

Aside from their constitutional role as presiding officers of the Senate, nineteenth-century vice presidents had no real power or authority. John Tyler, Millard Fillmore, Andrew Johnson, and Chester Arthur ascended to the presidency upon the deaths of William Henry Harrison, Zachary Taylor, Abraham Lincoln, and James Garfield, but their contributions as presidents did nothing to enhance the reputation of the vice presidency. None of the four distinguished himself in the White House (though Johnson did become the first president to be impeached). The assassination of William McKinley and the succession of Vice President Theodore Roosevelt to the presidency in 1901 began a slow but intermittent rehabilitation of the vice presidency. Roosevelt was a vocal and comparatively assertive vice president, and upon ascending to the Oval Office, he became one of America's most admired chief executives. His effectiveness as president finally alerted Americans to the potential importance of a historically neglected office.

Yet in the four decades following Roosevelt's presidency, the vice presidency again largely languished. The death of yet another president, Warren Harding, did not prove as fortuitous for his successor, not least because Calvin Coolidge was no Teddy Roosevelt (in fact, he was nicknamed "Silent Cal" due to his reluctance to speak when attending social functions). However, in 1945, the death of Franklin D. Roosevelt again catapulted a vice president into the political spotlight. Roosevelt's successor, Harry S. Truman, had served as vice president for only six months when he was sworn in as president. Roosevelt had selected Truman as his running mate in 1944 to replace Vice President Henry Wallace, who had come to be regarded as a political liability among conservative Democrats. Truman, the junior senator from Missouri, only saw Roosevelt three times between inauguration day and the day that the president died. The first time Truman even heard about the Manhattan Project and the existence of an atomic bomb was after he had been sworn in as president.

When Truman became president in April 1945, no one could have predicted that he would become the architect of America's national security state and one of its most formidable commanders in chief. Compared unfavorably to his former boss in almost every possible way by the public, Truman shattered those expectations and had an exceptionally consequential presidency, especially with respect to shaping American foreign policy in the post–World War II era.

Vice presidents today play a more significant role in the day-to-day operation of the White House. The growth in the responsibilities of the vice presidency arose not from constitutional articles or provisions but from presidential discretion. Like Cabinet directors, vice presidents are chosen for a variety of reasons. Presidential candidates choose running mates for geographic or ideological balance or for party unity. Those characteristics do not necessarily mean that the vice president is good at governing and management. However, over time, policy knowledge and management skills did become a larger factor, both in selecting vice presidential nominees and in expanding the vice president's role in the executive branch.

For example, during the 1950s, Dwight Eisenhower allowed his vice president, Richard Nixon, to attend Cabinet, National Security Council (NSC), and other legislative meetings. When Eisenhower was ill, Nixon presided over the meetings. Nixon was also the first vice president to have an office inside the White House. Much of Nixon's authority was in the area of foreign policy, as he had become well versed in many aspects of international affairs during his tenures in both the House of Representatives and the Senate prior to joining Eisenhower on the Republican ticket in 1952. Nixon even represented the administration on several foreign trips, including his famous "kitchen debates" with Soviet Premier Nikita Khrushchev at the American National Exhibition in Moscow in 1959. All of these responsibilities increased the visibility of an institution that had been relatively anonymous throughout the previous 150 years.

America's next vice president, Lyndon Johnson, participated frequently in legislative efforts of the Kennedy administration, which recognized that his political skills and contacts from his days as Senate Majority Leader were valuable. Yet Johnson was still not considered among the inner circle of advisors within the Kennedy administration. In fact, after Kennedy's election in 1960, Johnson assumed that his political career was mostly over. He spent much of his time as a roving international ambassador for the White House and had few policy responsibilities. Of course, his life changed dramatically when Kennedy was assassinated in November 1963 and Johnson was sworn in as America's 36th president.

Walter Mondale was the first vice president to achieve institutional power for the office. As noted in the staffing and cabinet discussions, access to the president is perhaps the most significant sign of power. Staff members who see the president frequently have more influence over the president's decision-making and deeper understandings of his priorities and attitudes than those who do not. Mondale had a large staff; he saw the president frequently, and in Jimmy Carter, he had a willing partner for expanding the role of the office. Thus, he was an active participant in addressing many issues confronting the Carter administration. He expanded the office well beyond its traditionally limited responsibilities, lobbying Congress on the administration's behalf, speaking on behalf of the White House to the public as well as interest groups, attending ceremonial functions in place of the president, and campaigning on behalf of fellow Democrats running for office. An active role for the vice president still ultimately depends on the approval of the president; however, political historians assert that Mondale permanently expanded the institutional capacity of the office.

George H. W. Bush played a similar role in the Reagan White House, meeting regularly with the president and providing Washington experience to a president who had served as governor of California, far from the nation's capital. Ironically, Bush's vice president, Dan Quayle, was just the opposite. Quayle was a relatively unknown senator from Indiana when Bush selected him to be his running mate. After their victory in the 1988 presidential election, however, Quayle became better known for public gaffes than having any significant role within the Bush White House.

Since then, the trend has been for increased activism, capacity, and management from the vice president. Recent vice presidents have all received extensive staff and continuous access to the president—and they have served presidents who were willing to rely on the vice president's skill and expertise in specific areas. As vice president in the Clinton White House from 1993 to 2001, Al Gore was intimately involved in policymaking, taking special interest in environmental issues, bureaucratic reform, and information technology. Gore was a trusted advisor to Clinton and an integral part of the administration. Dick Cheney, a hard-nosed, seasoned veteran of two previous Republican administrations, was George W. Bush's point person on national-security issues throughout Bush's two terms in office (2001–2009). Cheney had unprecedented authority over strategic planning and military operations, as well as substantial responsibility over diplomatic issues. However, critics considered Cheney's expansive exercise of power a worrisome precedent as he took the office well beyond the activities of his predecessors. His role, particularly in the early years of the Bush administration, has been described as that of a "surrogate chief of staff," "co-president," and "deputy president." Not only did Cheney manage the response to terror on the morning of 9/11 (Bush was at an education event in Florida), but he and his office were also involved in some of the most controversial decisions and events of the Bush administration. Cheney's vice presidential office played important roles in creating a domestic surveillance program, setting interrogation policies for detained suspected terrorists that some critics characterized as torture, and revealing the identity of a CIA agent who had been critical of the Bush Administration. Cheney also orchestrated Bush administration efforts in falsely linking Saddam Hussein to Al Qaeda and falsely claiming that Iraq possessed weapons of mass destruction. These claims helped build public support for the U.S. invasion of Iraq in 2003.

Joe Biden, who served as vice president during President Barack Obama's two terms in office (2009–2017), chose a relationship path with Obama modeled after the Gore-Clinton relationship. An experienced legislator with impressive foreign-policy credentials, Biden played significant roles in a wide range of political and policy areas in the Obama administration. On January 12, 2016, Obama awarded Biden the Medal of Freedom, with distinction, an honor previously awarded to few individuals. In his remarks, Obama highlighted how the twenty-first century vice presidency remains an expanded, influential part of the institution of the presidency.

After Donald Trump clinched the Republican presidential nomination in the summer of 2016, he selected Mike Pence as his running mate. Pence was a seasoned politician who served 12 years in the House of Representatives and one term as governor of Indiana before being tapped by Trump. He was viewed as an effective way to address possible voter concerns for which Trump had no prior political experience. In addition, Pence had tremendous credibility with social conservative voters regarded as a core constituency of the Republican Party. Since being sworn in as vice president in January 2017, Pence has played an important role in presidential-congressional relations, especially as a conduit to congressional Republicans (not all of whom are Trump supporters in private).

THE FIRST LADY

There is no constitutional role for the president's family, yet there is no avoiding the public role that is inevitable for anyone who is married to the president. For most of the country's history, the president's wife has served as a sort of unofficial hostess in chief. In the modern era, the duties of the first lady include some or all of the following: wife and mother, public figure and celebrity, the nation's social hostess, symbol of U.S. womanhood, White House manager and preservationist, campaigner, champion of social causes, presidential spokesperson, presidential and political party booster, diplomat, and political and presidential partner. As with the vice president, the extent to which the first lady adopts any or all of these roles depends on private negotiations with the president and, to some extent, public negotiations with the country.

The Office of the First Lady has become, in recent years, part of the official organizational structure of the Executive Office of the President. One of the main responsibilities of the first lady's staff is to manage day-to-day dealings with the news media. In addition to a press secretary, most first ladies of the modern era have also employed a chief of staff, a social secretary, a projects director (for causes that a first lady may adopt), and several other special assistants. Since the 1970s, first ladies have employed anywhere between 12 and 28 full-time employees for their staffs. First ladies also have an office in the White House, usually in the building's East Wing; to date, only one—Hillary Clinton—chose to have her office in the West Wing of the White House, where the Oval Office is also located. The location of Clinton's office was a clear indication of the important advisory role that she played within her husband's administration.

Given the prevailing attitudes toward women during most of the nation's history, the political assertiveness of first ladies has been a comparatively recent phenomenon. Yet there were two early exceptions to the rule. Abigail

Adams, wife of the second president, was observant of contemporary social graces. But she also was opinionated and firm, offering advice and counsel to her husband throughout his political career. Likewise, James Madison considered his wife Dolley an invaluable asset during his presidency. He relinquished control over the presidential residence to her and relied on her to coordinate the evacuation of the White House during the War of 1812.

The first presidential spouse, however, to truly break the mold of the First Lady as an ornament to the president was Edith Wilson. For all intents and purposes, she ran the presidency following Woodrow Wilson's stroke in 1919, earning the nickname "Mrs. President."

Like Edith Wilson, Eleanor Roosevelt was pushed into public service by unusual circumstances. Her husband, Franklin D. Roosevelt, contracted polio in 1921 and depended on his wife for his political survival thereafter. Eleanor Roosevelt campaigned vigorously for her husband, managed his schedule, acted as his closest advisor, and did as much as anyone to sustain the myth of a vigorous and healthy president. But she also emerged as a significant political figure in her own right. During her husband's presidency, she spoke out against sexism and discrimination, worked hard for the realization of lifelong progressive political goals, and transformed the purely ceremonial role of first lady into a substantive presence within the White House. From both a political and social perspective, Eleanor Roosevelt's accomplishments were formidable. As the first lady, her power rivaled that of her husband's key aides and cabinet secretaries, demonstrating an influence over the president that was rare for anyone, especially the president's wife.

Since that time, the public role for first ladies has mostly been a social one, yet several first ladies since Eleanor Roosevelt's tenure provide distinct examples of the power and influence that can come with being the first spouse. Both Rosalynn Carter and Hillary Clinton opted for active involvement in policy decisions and publicly acknowledged their political role within their husband's administration. Carter became an advocate for numerous causes, most notably research on mental health issues. At the request of her husband, she also sat in on cabinet and other policy meetings, acted as one of his closest advisors, and even served as an envoy abroad in Latin America and other areas. Clinton, perhaps rivaling only Eleanor Roosevelt in the politically significant role that she would play in her husband's administration, was a successful attorney and longtime advocate for children's issues before moving into the White House. As first lady, she acted as one of Bill Clinton's top policy advisors and most notably headed up the Clinton administration's health care reform policy initiative (first introduced in 1993, but which failed to achieve congressional approval in 1994). After the failure with health care reform, Clinton lowered her political profile and embraced more traditional activities for a first lady, as well as focused on social issues, particularly those dealing with women and children. After the Clintons left the White House, Hillary Clinton pursued an active and high-profile political career, serving eight years as a U.S. Senator from New York and four years as Secretary of State (2009–2013). She also ran for the presidency in 2008 (when she lost the Democratic nomination to Obama) and again in 2016 (when she won the Democratic nomination but lost in the general election).

Other first ladies, such as Mamie Eisenhower, Lady Bird Johnson, Barbara Bush, and Laura Bush, opted for a more traditional, nonpublic role in their husband's White House. Regardless of the public versus private role of the first lady, several have played unique roles in their husband's administrations. Jackie Kennedy, a former debutante, is remembered for her trendsetting fashions, redecorating the aging White House, bringing art and culture into Washington political circles, and providing glamour to the Kennedy administration at the start of the television age of politics. Betty Ford was an outspoken advocate for women's rights, including passage of the Equal Rights Amendment, and she is also remembered for raising public consciousness about addiction by acknowledging her own problems with alcohol. Although mostly a traditional first lady while in the public eye, Nancy Reagan was a formidable presence in the Reagan White House in protecting her husband's best interests. The president trusted her judgment supremely and even consulted her regarding staffing decisions in the White House and major policy objectives.

Michelle Obama, a Princeton and Harvard-educated attorney who put her career on hold during her husband's presidential campaign in 2008, chose the more traditional role of first lady by supporting nonpolitical causes such as support for military families and fighting childhood obesity. And, like several of her predecessors, she also raised two young daughters while living in the White House. In the 2016 presidential campaign, she stepped out of her nonpartisan role to campaign extensively for Hillary Clinton. Her 2016 convention speech in support of Clinton's nomination was widely acclaimed.

Melania Trump is also raising a young son in the White House. A former model and native of Slovenia, she is only the second first lady not born in the United States (Louisa Adams, wife of John Quincy Adams, was born in London) and the first to be a naturalized citizen and for whom English is not her native language. In 2018, Melania Trump launched her "Be Best" initiative, a public awareness campaign focused on the well-being for youth that advocates against cyberbullying and drug use.

CONCLUSION

The president's relationship with the many departments, agencies, and officials within the executive branch is both simple and complex. As the chief executive officer of the American government, the president is similar to the CEO of a major corporation in that they are the boss. Yet, unlike a private corporation, the American government employs more than three million people, most of whom are civil servants (though the top positions within each agency are political appointees). While the organizational structure of Congress may seem complicated with its many committees and subcommittees, it pales in comparison to the executive branch and its large and wide-reaching bureaucracy.

It is ultimately the job of the president to coordinate and control the bureaucracy as it interprets and implements public policy. The president, who takes an oath to faithfully execute the laws as well as to preserve, protect, and defend the Constitution, has various tools to help him achieve this task. They include top government officials within the Cabinet and other agencies, the White House Staff, as well as institutional mechanisms such as executive orders, signing statements, and budgetary and regulatory review. Not all presidents, however, have shown skills in organizing and managing the executive branch, and though this task consumes the biggest part of his time while in office, presidents rarely receive recognition in keeping the federal government functioning on a day-to-day basis.

7

The President and Policymaking

In 1936, political scientist Harold Lasswell wrote his classic work *Politics: Who Gets What, When, How,* in which he described the ways in which political influence determines how political resources are distributed. In a nutshell, that is what policymaking at any level of government is all about—there are limited resources to pursue various policies and initiatives, and many political actors engage in a competition to make their ideas and goals the ones driving the legislative agenda. A president is just one political actor in this equation; not only does he have to compete with the other two coequal branches of the federal government but also state and local governments, political parties, interest groups, and the news media are but a few of the other political actors involved in policymaking. Perhaps the most important participant in this process is the American public; after all, in the U.S. government, the people are sovereign (meaning that they, ultimately, hold all the power). While many look to the president to determine and pursue policies in the interest of the American public, there are often more opportunities for failure than success along the way.

This chapter considers the president's role in all areas of policymaking—domestic, economic, and foreign. As the previous chapters have shown, there are many limitations to presidential power by constitutional design. Yet, some presidents, in certain situations, have nonetheless managed to oversee consequential changes to the American system of government. As also noted, much of the key policymaking activity exists outside the president's control. In domestic and economic policymaking, the president can significantly influence the agenda, but he can rarely exercise much control over the central actors or the context of the policy environment. Exceptions have occurred, however, in times of national crisis, such as the 9/11 terrorist attacks in 2001 or the global coronavirus pandemic in 2020. Presidents tend to have more latitude in foreign policy, although often the White House also responds to major world events over which it has no or limited influence.

DOMESTIC POLICY LEADERSHIP

While on the campaign trail, presidential candidates make lots of promises to voters about what they will do if elected. While most presidents at least attempt to change or create new domestic policies, accomplishing those goals is a difficult task. As a result, modern presidents often focus primarily on foreign policy and secondarily on economic policy, at the expense of domestic policy. This is mainly so because change in the domestic policy arena is difficult to achieve. As the commander in chief as well as the nation's leader on the world stage, presidents have more opportunities to respond to foreign and economic matters while domestic policy issues require more coordination with Congress and states. To enact changes, a president must deal with Congress, direct the responses of the large federal bureaucracy that is implementing the policy, and respond to budgetary constraints. Domestic policy is also complex. Experts are required in numerous policy areas to handle the diverse policy needs. Few members of Congress, even those who serve for decades, develop policy expertise that allows them to understand the nuts and bolts of how to implement laws and programs once created. While the executive branch does have policy expertise within the various departments and agencies, the political environment can make it difficult for a president to gain traction regarding domestic policy changes.

How does a president set the domestic policy agenda once elected? Beyond the campaign promises made, the political environment plays a large role in guiding White House action.

Various factors come into play, including public attitudes as well as expectations. An important legacy from Franklin D. Roosevelt's presidency, however, still casts a long shadow over public expectations of the president. Ever since Roosevelt made a point of highlighting the Depression-fighting actions his administration took during his first 100 days in office, the media has demonstrated an obsession with monitoring the first 100 days of every subsequent administration. No other president has faced a crisis of that scale upon assuming office, and no president has passed as much legislation, yet the expectation that a new president will pass major new domestic initiatives right out of the gate exists nonetheless. The state of the economy is also a significant factor that shapes the political environment. Since 1940, there have been only 12 years in which the federal government operated with a budget surplus. Deficit spending makes it harder for a president to create new programs, hire more federal employees, and service more constituencies.

The president is involved in all stages of the domestic policy cycle; however, the influence of the president sits primarily with the ability to set the agenda and the extent to which he can manage the capacity of the government to affect policy. Through both enumerated and implied constitutional powers, the president is uniquely positioned to set both the public agenda (through the media) and the government's agenda (by recommending legislation to Congress). Since the policymaking environment straddles the executive, legislative, and judicial branches, as well as state and local government and the private sector, the primary goal for the president is coordination across issues, actors, and institutions, while a secondary goal is to obtain policy expertise. The president's domestic policy experts serve in the Executive Office of the President; however, there are also individuals outside the administration who influence policy outcomes as well as the president's ability to get things done on his policy agenda.

White House policy experts come from universities, think tanks, and policymaking positions in other levels of government or remain in place from earlier administrations. The policy experts in the White House primarily work in the policy councils. These are the real workhorses behind presidential domestic policy, and their contributions enable the transition from political goals and adoption of strategies to actionable programs based on actual circumstances. They compile data, perform analyses, prepare strategy, provide expertise, and fulfill any number of other jobs assigned to them by the president or his staff. The primary office for domestic policy in the White House is the Domestic Policy Council (DPC), which handles most areas of domestic policy except law enforcement, drug interdiction, and scientific research. Outside of the White House, numerous individuals, organizations, and institutions influence the ability of the president to shape domestic policy. Within the government, Congress dominates policymaking, but governors and other governmental entities can have influence. Powerful interest groups and members of the private sector also play an influential role in the process.

Since the New Deal rolled out by Roosevelt and the Great Society programs of Lyndon B. Johnson's administration, domestic policy agendas have increased the role that the presidency plays in many aspects of citizens' lives.

The most important category within the domestic policy arena is social services. It is also the most resource-intensive, as it accounts for most domestic federal spending and a sizable share of the domestic federal work force. These programs encompass assistance for the socioeconomically dislocated and disadvantaged, social security, health care, education, and many other areas. This aspect of the president's domestic policy agenda has steadily grown since the 1930s. These programs include Social Security; Medicare; Medicaid; health care coverage; and services for the disabled, America's veterans, dependent children, and students. The most expansive growth in this area occurred with the passage of the New Deal agenda, including social-service and regulatory measures affecting workers, employers, farmers, utilities, banks, consumer prices, wages, natural resources, as well as efforts to increase consumer purchasing power and capabilities through programs for dislocated minorities, industrial workers, retired persons, and others disproportionately affected by the Great Depression.

As significant as most New Deal programs were, no single initiative has been as closely associated with the New Deal as the Social Security Act. This law, enacted in 1935, created a guaranteed federal pension for the elderly and established unemployment compensation, aid for dependent children, support for unwed mothers, and related social welfare services. Maintaining the financial viability of Social Security for future generations has become an enduring challenge for presidents, as changes in retirement ages as well as increased life expectancy have greatly expanded the size of this entitlement program. The growth in federal spending on Social Security has made it a major part of the overall federal budget. Similarly, programs launched during Johnson's Great Society initiatives of the 1960s expanded assistance for the poor, the elderly, the young, political and social minorities, and mothers. These various measures produced significant changes in American workplaces, schools, housing, cities, and more.

One of the most prominent parts of the Great Society was the War on Poverty, which sought to provide better living conditions and better economic and educational opportunities to those living in poverty. The creation of Medicare in 1965 provided health care benefits to retired persons that included hospital treatment, nursing home subsidies, and physician care. Also created was Medicaid, a joint program with the states to help meet the medical needs of the poor, disabled, elderly not eligible for Medicare, dependent children and unwed mothers, and others identified as needy by federal or state governments. Johnson also created the Office of Economic Opportunity (OEO) with agencies to provide job training, housing assistance, educational enrichment, food and clothing subsidies, basic health care, resources for neighborhood improvement, and other services.

The presidents who followed Johnson were mostly unable to replicate his success creating new, large entitlement programs. Not only did budgetary restraints exist but also few opportunities existed as so many policy areas were already covered at the federal level. Richard Nixon, working with a Democratic Congress, expanded a few Great Society welfare programs (such as food stamps and other benefits to low-income Americans), while Ronald Reagan made cutting spending for such domestic programs a hallmark of his 1980 presidential campaign (and decreased spending in this area during his first term in office). A challenge that several Democratic and Republican presidents tried to tackle, dating back to Theodore Roosevelt, was providing health care coverage for most, if not all, Americans. Bill Clinton campaigned in 1992 on many domestic policy issues, including the promise to enact major health care reform. A task force headed by first lady Hillary Clinton created a complex policy proposal to expand health care coverage, but it failed to secure passage in Congress in 1994. Major reforms of health care would wait until 2010, when Barack Obama pushed through the single largest entitlement program since the New Deal—the Affordable Care Act (also known as Obamacare).

Beyond social services, law enforcement is another major domestic policy concern for presidents. This policy area encompasses federal anticrime initiatives, border security and immigration, homeland security and domestic counterterrorism, and civil-rights protections. By the turn of the twentieth century, as the complexities of industrialization and urbanization coupled with continued population growth created a demand for a more active federal law-enforcement role, not to mention the increasing number of federal laws, the executive branch acquired increasing duties and responsibilities. For the modern presidency, issues such as immigration, border security, drug interdiction, and civil-rights protection have become among the most important priorities for American voters. The most obvious aspect of law-enforcement policy is crime prevention. Agencies such as the Justice Departments' Federal Bureau of Investigation (FBI) and Drug Enforcement Administration (DEA); the Department of Homeland Security's (DHS) Bureau of Alcohol, Tobacco, Firearms, and Explosives (ATF); and the Secret Service provide essential crime prevention and criminal investigation services. Most of the nation's crime prevention and criminal investigations resources, however, are housed in state, county, and municipal agencies.

Law enforcement policy also includes immigration, which is under the supervision of DHS. One of the most divisive issues of the last 30 years, immigration is not confined to worries about terrorist and criminal infiltration into the United States. The real issue has been illegal immigration, which has become a volatile political topic and one for which presidents of both parties have been unable to find a bipartisan solution. George W. Bush offered a compromise solution that was not much different from what Obama would propose a few years later, but it was neither stringent enough for mainstream Republicans nor sufficiently welcoming for Democrats.

Trump promised throughout the 2016 presidential campaign to "build a wall" to crack down on illegal immigration. He signed several executive orders within his first weeks in office related to this issue, yet lasting reform through bipartisan congressional legislation has remained elusive.

Environmental protection, climate change, and energy policies ranging from drilling for natural gas and oil on federal lands to tax breaks for "clean energy" industries are also important yet polarizing domestic policy issues that challenge presidents. Disasters and controversies such as the 1989 Exxon Valdez oil spill in Alaska, the Deepwater Horizon oil spill in 2010, and a multi-year legal fight over construction of the "Keystone XL Pipeline," a proposed oil pipeline to transport Canadian oil through several American states for development, have all thrust energy and environmental policy into the spotlight at various times. But otherwise, environmental policy has not attracted much in the way of front page headlines since the early 1970s, when widespread air and water pollution along with pesticide contamination had become so obvious that they could not be ignored any longer. The Nixon administration responded to these threats with the creation of the Environmental Protection Agency (EPA), while a new generation of environmental activists agitated for appropriate reforms and regulations at all levels.

Environmental protection took a back seat to economic expansion and industrial productivity during the Reagan years, however, and environmental regulation was increasingly framed by Republicans as the enemy of economic progress and free enterprise. Gradually, however, and despite many partisan differences on the issue, both the American public and the broader global community became aware of large-scale problems such as climate change and the degradation of the earth's atmosphere.

In addition to environmental policy, energy policy has been a prominent aspect of domestic agendas for a few decades. During the 1970s, the Arab oil embargo and the by now discredited calculations that the global supply of fossil fuels could be depleted in as little as 100 years caused widespread worries among policymakers and the public. In the late 1970s, Jimmy Carter was the first president to devote considerable attention to the future development of alternative fuels, and he also decried the country's dependence on foreign oil. No other issue on Carter's domestic agenda received as much attention from the White House as the president's national energy plan. By the 1980s, an economic recovery, substantial gains in fuel efficiency, and more realistic estimates about the world's energy supplies eased the country's anxiety about fossil fuels. Since then, energy policy has become a matter of economic sustainability and national security, and reducing American's dependence on foreign sources of oil has been a goal of both Democratic and Republican presidents, though the two parties often differ on how to achieve that goal.

ECONOMIC POLICY LEADERSHIP

The state of the economy can play a crucial role in presidential leadership. Important political matters when dealing with economic policies include efforts to balance the federal budget, the national debt, the appropriate rate of taxation for businesses and different socioeconomic groups, and federal spending on domestic programs. Many presidents have had to consider economic stimulus packages, and policy in this area can vary greatly depending on the ideological views of the president. Since the 1980s, Republican presidents have campaigned on and signed major tax cuts, including Reagan, George W. Bush, and Trump. Yet all three also saw deficit spending increase the national debt substantially during their time in office. Democratic presidents do not tend to make tax cuts a major part of their legislative agenda, but their support for expansion of domestic programs can increase the national debt as well.

Presidents rely on four major players in the area of economic policy: the Department of Treasury, the Office of Management and Budget (OMB), the Council of Economic Advisors (CEA), and the Federal Reserve Board. Treasury is one of the original four cabinets, and the secretary is next in line after the Secretary of State for presidential succession. Treasury has a large staff and substantial budget and handles such matters as tax collection and disbursement of funds for the federal government, debt management, financial institutions and markets, and international trade. Secretaries of the Treasury tend to come from corporate or financial backgrounds. For example, Trump's Treasury secretary, Steve Mnuchin, is a former hedge fund manager who spent the bulk of his career at Goldman Sachs (Clinton's second Treasury Secretary, Robert Rubin, also had a long career at Goldman Sachs, which is one of the largest investment banks in the world).

The OMB, created in 1921, gained prominence as a presidential tool for economic policy during the New Deal era and continued throughout the 1960s as the federal government continued to grow (due to expanding domestic programs as well as the increased governmental resources devoted to the Cold War). OMB responsibilities include the development of the budget submitted to Congress and to serve as a clearinghouse for legislation to ensure compliance with the president's budget priorities. By the mid-1960s, the agency's emphasis began to shift to provide more management skills for the president in the area of budgetary matters and less legislative authority, as more policy decisions were moving into distinct offices within the White House. Budget directors are political appointees and speak for the president on economic matters.

The CEA was created in 1946 by a congressional act to provide government leadership over the national economy. The three council members are economists and are aided by other economists on the staff to provide advice to the president on economic matters. The theory is that these economists have no other ties to any other economic agencies, and therefore, they can give the president candid advice. Most are academics and do not have political backgrounds.

The Federal Reserve, which is the central banking system of the United States, was created in 1913 to regulate the supply of money and credit. The Chairman of "The Fed" is appointed by the president and represents the bank in public speeches, at international conferences, and in congressional testimony. The Fed controls the money supply in three ways: it buys and sells government securities, it sets the discount rate (the interest it charges banks to which it makes loans), and it stipulates the amount of money that federal reserve banks must hold as reserves.

Presidents sometimes need to choose between what is best for the economy in the short or long term and weigh that against what is best for their political career in the short and long term. Presidents can benefit politically when the economy is strong and can be limited in what they can do during economic recessions. For example, George H. W. Bush's decision in 1990 to support an increase in taxes (after his infamous "read my lips" pledge not to do so at the 1988 Republican National Convention) signaled his desire to cope with the impending recession (which meant increasing spending) rather than focus on the increasing deficit (which meant reducing spending).

In spite of the numerous domestic issues that Clinton campaigned on in 1992, highlighted by the campaign mantra "It's the economy, stupid," the major focus of his economic package in 1993 became deficit reduction, which would lower long-term interest rates to benefit the economy. Without a strong economy and economic growth, many domestic policy proposals are not possible. Also, spending cuts and tax increases are never popular with voters and can be a tricky political proposition.

FOREIGN POLICY LEADERSHIP

As political scientist Aaron Wildavsky famously argued, there are "two presidencies"—one dealing with domestic policy and the other concerned with foreign policy. Wildavsky made this argument during the first two decades of the Cold War, suggesting that presidents prefer to focus on foreign over domestic policy because they have more constitutional and statutory authority and can act more decisively without congressional interference. While the theory is not as accurate today, as Congress has become more involved in the development of foreign policy, Wildavsky's observation is nonetheless instructive when considering the expansion of presidential powers in the foreign policy arena. Governed by a group of actors that includes the president, his staff and advisors, legislators, lobbyists, international organizations, foreign governments, all reflecting national strategic priorities and political ideals, foreign and defense policymaking is a major focus of presidential politics.

Executive branch policymaking in this area is created through various groups, including the Department of Defense (with 1.5 million uniformed personnel and 750,000 civilian employees), the Department of Homeland Security, the Joint Chiefs of Staff, and the Central Intelligence Agency. In addition, the National Security Council is a senior group of officials chaired by the president, with a chief advisor and a staff composed of foreign policy experts. The State Department, which employs about 5,000 professional diplomats, is responsible for the implementation of policy rather than the coordination of policy for the White House.

Other strategic considerations come through America's role in military alliances such as the North Atlantic Treaty Organization (NATO), which was established after World War II to keep the Soviets out of Western Europe. As of 2020, the membership of NATO consisted of 30 nations across North America and Europe. The United States is also one of five permanent members of the United Nations Security Council, along with Britain, France, Russia, and China. The United States was a leader in the formation of the UN in 1945 and is its major financial backer, though presidents have varied in their support for the organization. Some conservative critics have argued that the United States pays an unfair share of the organization's operating costs and that the nation's foreign policy objectives should never be subordinate to the goals of the UN member nations.

Prior to World War II, the United States was mostly an isolationist country (with the obvious exception of World War I), avoiding a large role in world affairs. Since then, the United States has taken an expansive internationalist view as a global superpower. With the end of World War II in 1945, U.S. foreign and defense policies were driven by a doctrine of containment against the Soviet Union and the spread of communism. Harry Truman viewed the Soviet Union as an aggressor that wanted global domination. This led to the "Cold War," which lasted 45 years before the collapse of the Soviet Union in the early 1990s. No actual combat occurred between American and Soviet forces during this time, but both countries were locked in a state of deep-seated hostility. During the late 1940s and through the 1950s, Presidents Truman and Eisenhower supported policies that sought to repel Soviet expansion of influence into various parts of the globe. For example, the Truman Doctrine focused on American aid in countries such as Turkey and Greece, and the Eisenhower Doctrine focused on aid to countries in the Middle East, which supported the view that America would help aid any countries that would follow the path of democracy.

Military action during the Cold War included U.S. involvement in Korea and Vietnam. The Korean War began in 1950 when North Korea (with the support of the Soviet Union and China) invaded South Korea (aided by the United Nations, with most support coming from the United States). Truman believed that sending American troops to fight the spread of communism was an important strategic priority during the early years of the Cold War. The Korean War ended in stalemate in 1953 just months after Dwight Eisenhower's election. More than 40,000 Americans died in the conflict, and the stalemate between South Korea and its communist neighbor to the north remains intact. American troops have remained in South Korea ever since, for the country continues to be regarded as an important economic, military, and diplomatic ally of the United States.

The longest and most debilitating conflict of the Cold War for the United States, both in terms of casualties and loss of international prestige, was the Vietnam War. Nearly 60,000 Americans died in the war, which stemmed from a so-called Domino Theory that was embraced by many American foreign policymakers in post–World War II era. The Domino Theory assumed that, because key geopolitical regions were precariously balanced between communism and anticommunism and, by extension, between Soviet and American spheres of influence, a marginal increase in Soviet influence in a particular region would lead to the eventual communist takeover of the whole region. In other words, once a strategically significant state in such a region fell to communism, the rest of the states in that region would follow like dominos.

The Vietnam War spanned six American presidencies. American involvement in Vietnam began as early as 1946 during the Truman administration, and Gerald Ford was the president when the war ended with the capture of Saigon by the communist Viet Cong forces in 1975. Despite clear American military superiority, the Vietnam War was a failure by almost every measure. Most importantly, it was the first war the United States ever lost and, especially to its critics, a conspicuous repudiation of the Domino Theory and much of the rationale for U.S. military intervention during the Cold War. Massively unpopular at home by the late 1960s, the war produced civil unrest and protests in scores of American cities and created mistrust and skepticism in the American public regarding federal governance, which are still felt today. In terms of foreign policy, Vietnam demonstrated the difficulties associated with nation-building as a military objective. It also greatly diminished American willingness to intervene in foreign conflicts that did not invoke a compelling U.S. interest or present a clear and definite exit strategy.

During the early 1970s, Nixon began a policy of détente, a period of relaxed tensions and improved relations between the United States and the

Soviet Union, at the same time that he launched a slow withdrawal of American forces out of Vietnam. He also made a historic trip to China in 1972, becoming the first president to visit the country, which had become communist in 1949, while in office. During the 1980s, after the Soviet invasion of Afghanistan in 1979, détente with the Soviet Union ended, and Reagan called for a more hard-line view toward the Soviet Union, which he described as an "evil empire." This led, in part, to the massive American defense buildups of the decade. The Soviet Union collapsed in December 1991, ending the Cold War and creating what George H. W. Bush called a "new world order" multilateralism, which means nations acting together in response to problems and crises.

Heading a multinational coalition, the United States invaded Iraq in January of 1991 to liberate Kuwait, which had been violently annexed by Iraqi military forces. Though this first "Gulf War" was brief and limited in scope, continued American involvement in the region was not. Through the United Nations, the United States and its allies became guarantors of stability in Kuwait and other swaths of the Middle East, which required an ongoing commitment of American resources for the next several years. Closer to home, Bush ordered the invasion of Panama in December 1989 to capture the military dictator Manuel Noriega, a reputed supporter of regional terrorist organizations and narcotics trafficker. In other troubled areas of the world, particularly Somalia, the Bush administration intervened for humanitarian reasons, but regional political and military instability eventually undermined the U.S.-led campaign.

Clinton was not as eager to commit American military resources abroad, and the continued American geopolitical dominance was not always a top priority for his administration. The Clinton administration, dominated by baby boomers who witnessed the failures of nation-building and interventionism during their formative years, limited U.S. diplomatic and particularly military engagements to situations that invoked a clear national interest or moral imperative. The Clinton years were noteworthy for reliance on the Powell Doctrine, named after the president's Chairman of the Joint Chiefs of Staff, Colin Powell. He advocated American military involvement only in those cases with a compelling national interest at stake, a limited engagement, minimal political entanglements, and a recognizable exit strategy. This was a policy, for example, that guided U.S. intervention in the former Yugoslavia and strikes against tactical targets in Iraq during Clinton's two terms in office.

The terrorist attacks against the United States on 9/11 caused a wholesale reformulation of American foreign policy by the George W. Bush administration. The Powell Doctrine was set aside (even though Powell was serving as Secretary of State at the time) and was replaced by the so-called War on Terror. Launched shortly after the terrorist attacks, this

"War" ultimately secured a policy of preemptive action against rogue states and organizations, and as per its neoconservative supporters, it also justified foreign intervention for the promotion and protection of liberal-democratic principles (known as the Bush Doctrine). Consequently, military intervention in Afghanistan and Iraq and a hawkish posture toward Iran and North Korea, both part of what Bush identified as an "axis of evil," were justified by the need to protect American interests and support the consolidation of liberal democracy abroad.

In another reversal, Obama rejected the Bush Doctrine and attempted to distance himself and his administration from what he perceived as the foreign policy excesses of his predecessor. Unfortunately, like many before him, Obama learned quickly that reversals of foreign policy, though warranted and defensible in many cases, are not always achievable. Prevailing geopolitical realities kept Obama from doing what he had wished and promised. Under Obama, the United States maintained a significant number of troops in Iraq, though he implemented a gradual reduction of forces until the official end of the war in December 2011. Subsequent destabilization in both Afghanistan and Iraq also convinced Obama to once again increase American troop levels in both countries. In a move that was reminiscent of the early stages of the Vietnam war, however, these Americans were often labeled as "advisors" or something similar. As many presidents before him, Trump inherited many foreign policy initiatives with the decision to continue or alter course. Trump's major foreign policy initiatives have involved national security and fighting terrorism; he became the first president to visit North Korea in 2019.

In addition to national security, foreign policy also focuses on the security and promotion of national and strategic interests abroad, which includes economic objectives, assets, and opportunities. Recent presidents have devoted considerable attention to international trade and the coordination of multinational economic initiatives. Prior to the Reagan administration, allegiance to free trade and globalization was inconsistent. While encouraging the easing of trade barriers in some industries, especially in Western markets, most presidents before the 1980s could not let go of protectionist policies that favored American commodities and manufactured goods produced in domestic industries believed to be vulnerable to foreign competition. While some aspects of protectionism still survive, the commitment to free trade has dominated international economic policy for several decades. The minimization and abolition of tariffs, subsidies, quotas, dumping, and other practices that distort international markets have been goals of the last several presidents—Reagan, Clinton, Obama, and Trump particularly. However, they have at times encountered considerable opposition from lawmakers, blue-collar workers in American industries with significant international competition or manufacturing capacity, and anti-globalization advocates. Surprisingly, critics received a sympathetic ear from George W. Bush, whose instinct was to protect the auto, steel, mining, and banking industries, while Obama was a steadier and more enthusiastic supporter of free-trade deals than many Republicans, who have been the traditional advocates of free trade. Despite variable though consistent support since the early 1980s, globalization—a consequence of free trade that includes political, economic, and cultural integration—has been a tough sell. Its detractors have viewed it as the domination and enrichment of multinational firms at the expense of the middle class and American labor.

Modern presidents have increasingly concentrated on negotiating trade deals and lobbying international trade organizations. The General Agreement on Tariffs and Trade (GATT, in place from 1948 to 1995), and then replaced by the creation of the World Trade Organization (WTO) in 1995, is devoted to the reduction of tariffs, subsidies, quotas, and other trade barriers. They have proven useful to presidential administrations as a forum for the promotion of American goods and services. Still, because of their cumbersome size and limited abilities of these and similar institutions to produce results, presidents have tended to see them more as avenues for debate and deliberation than as instruments of tangible change. Clinton was a notable exception. He pressed hard for the creation of WTO, viewing it as a useful arena for the dissemination of American economic ideas, which he believed would facilitate international economic integration and the spread of democratic governance.

Institutions such as GATT and WTO, often lacking any authority to enact rules, such as the Group of Seven (G7) richest industrialized economies, Organization for Economic Cooperation and Development (OECD), Asia-Pacific Economic Cooperation (APEC), and others, have proven marginally effective at advancing concrete goals instead of abstract principles. On the other hand, multilateral and bilateral free-trade pacts have been pursued aggressively by recent American presidents. To negotiate quickly and more effectively, most presidents have asked Congress for so-called fast-track authority, renamed trade promotion authority (TPA) in 2002, to move quickly on trade agreements. TPA banned Congress from engaging in filibusters and adding amendments to trade deals. Under TPA, Congress was only given authority for up-or-down votes.

The most visible, and possibly most controversial, free-trade pact has been the North American Free Trade Agreement (NAFTA) between the United States, Canada, and Mexico. George H.W. Bush expended great effort to negotiate the deal in the concluding months of his presidency, though it was not ratified until 1994, nearly two years into the Clinton presidency. NAFTA resulted in the immediate elimination of tariffs on half of Mexican exports and more than one-third of U.S. exports. Given the concerns about its allegedly negative impact on the environment and American workers, however, NAFTA was not universally supported.

The proposed Free Trade Area of the Americas (FTAA), which was supposed to expand NAFTA to all North, Central, and South American countries except Cuba, has never materialized. In 2019, however, Trump (who during the 2016 campaign called NAFTA "the worst trade deal ever") signed into law the United States-Mexico-Canada Agreement (USMCA), which updates various provisions of NAFTA including intellectual property, the sale of American cars, and giving American farmers greater access to markets in Canada, among others. Trump also signed an executive order withdrawing the United States from the Trans-Pacific trade Partnership (TPP) during his first week in office in January 2017. The TPP had been the Obama administration's signature trade deal. Trump said that his withdrawal decision stemmed from his preference for negotiating trade deals one on one with specific countries.

Finally, human rights have been a major foreign policy issue for presidents in recent decades. The end of the Cold War changed the way the United States dealt with many former Soviet-allied countries in terms of national security and trade and economic issues, and this also brought human rights into the political forefront. These issues were often overlooked during the Cold War as U.S. policy concentrated primarily on containment. But with the "new world order" came greater recognition of human rights abuses among nations that the United States was now dealing with as part of the global marketplace and worldwide community.

Clinton was one of the staunchest and most diligent advocates of human rights that ever occupied the White House. He tried almost everything at his disposal to curtail widespread human rights abuses, including pressing for U.N. and unilateral U.S. sanctions, leveraging the rhetorical power of the presidency, and withholding aid. Similarly, George W. Bush and Obama were fierce critics of human rights abuses. Aside from using unilateral sanctions, they brought pressure on rogue regimes through the U.N. General Assembly, Security Council, and United Nations Human Rights Council (UNHRC). However, their efforts were only marginally effective. Vetoes by permanent security council members China and Russia upended numerous otherwise promising resolutions and encouraged them to use their veto powers as a bargaining chip against unsympathetic resolutions.

Compromises between human rights and stability have provided a rationale for many presidents in both parties to support authoritarian governments in various regions of the world. This is especially true in the case of countries such as China, Pakistan, and Russia. These countries, particularly China, are geopolitically significant in some way, and keeping these countries on good terms with the West has been a critical consideration for many administrations. China, for example, is the second largest economy in the world, the most populous nation on earth, and a growing military and diplomatic power. A certain amount of diplomacy (or what some would call appeasement) is necessary because of its effect on the global economy, its growing militarism and geopolitical assertiveness, and the desire to take advantage of Chinese markets, yet China's human rights record is dismal.

CONCLUSION

The common phrase that "elections have consequences" is never truer than when considering the president's role in policymaking. As the chief executive who is constitutionally charged with the task of recommending legislation to Congress, presidents are at times the most consequential actor within domestic policymaking, even if they have little control over the process. Regarding economic policy, presidents are often at the mercy of the ups and downs of the financial markets and global economic conditions; they benefit politically when the U.S. economy is strong and can have diminished opportunities for leadership during economic downturns.

Due to the expansion of the modern presidency, as well as the increased role of the United States on the global stage during the past century, the presidential role in foreign policy has expanded tremendously since World War II. Truth be told, while some presidents may look like they prefer focusing on one area of policy over another, all presidents must juggle the responsibilities of pursuing and implementing domestic, economic, and foreign policies simultaneously. Thanks to elections every four years and term limits, presidents come and go with regularity, but many policies that are implemented have a lasting impact beyond any one administration.

Conclusion: The Future of the American Presidency

On November 8, 2016, Donald J. Trump shocked the political world with an unexpected upset defeat of Hillary Clinton to win the presidential election. Few political pundits had given Trump, the real estate developer and reality television star, any chance of defeating Clinton, the former first lady, U.S. senator, and secretary of state. Nearly every poll, prediction, and statistical model showed that Clinton would win the presidency; nearly every other metric used by the news media showed that Trump would not, and could not, win. The reasons were numerous—Trump had few paths to win the Electoral College; he had no political or military experience; he had lied numerous times during the presidential campaign; he endured several scandals, including the release of a 2005 video where Trump can be heard discussing what many considered sexual assault against women; he was unpresidential and politically incorrect; his negatives (as in polling that showed how unpopular he was) were higher than any previous presidential candidate . . . the list went on and on among the political and media establishment. Yet, Trump still won the Electoral College and thus the presidency on Election Day.

While presidential legacies take decades to fully develop, and while many more lessons about the Trump presidency are sure to unfold, there is one thing that Trump has reminded us about the American system of government—despite the relative stability provided by the U.S. Constitution, when it comes to politics, anything can happen. For example, Trump is the first president with no prior political or military experience. But he is not the first president to win the Electoral College despite losing the popular vote. John Quincy Adams in 1824, Rutherford B. Hayes in 1876, Benjamin Harrison in 1888, and George W. Bush in 2000 lost the popular vote as well, though Trump's loss to Clinton by more than 3 million votes is certainly the highest number ever in that category. While Trump supporters applaud his unconventional method of governing, including his incessant use of Twitter, those opposed to Trump or his policies remain focused on resisting him at every turn. Both camps would probably agree, however, that Trump has disrupted the normal patterns that had existed in presidential politics for several decades.

THE POLITICAL ENVIRONMENT

Various factors help to shape the political environment, which in turn helps to determine much about the American presidency—most importantly, who runs for office, who wins, and ultimately, how the president governs. While Trump's presidency to date provides various data points for scholars to assess, Barack Obama's presidency also provides an excellent case study of the challenges of navigating (sometimes successfully while other times not) the political environment, the tasks of governing, and public expectations for presidents (as individuals) and the presidency (as a political institution).

Obama's 2008 campaign for the presidency was historic on many fronts. An excellent campaigner and eloquent public speaker, Obama beat the presumptive Democratic nominee (Hillary Clinton) in the primaries and a seasoned Washington politician (John McCain) in the general election. In doing so, he became the first president of color in American history. He did so through record-breaking fundraising; the most successful ground game perhaps ever witnessed in American politics; and strong outreach efforts to new, young, and independent voters. Obama's message of "hope and change," along with his signature campaign message of "yes we can," inspired millions. A political star was born during that campaign, but then came the irony of how Americans elect their presidents—once the winning candidate is sworn into office, the excitement of the campaign fades into the day-to-day task of governing. And effective governance often requires a different set of skills than effective campaigning.

Obama faced several urgent policy issues upon taking office, including the "Great Recession" plaguing the country as well as the two wars he inherited (in Afghanistan and Iraq). Initially, the narrative was more about how transformative Obama's presidency would be and which presidential icon (Franklin D. Roosevelt, John F. Kennedy, or Ronald Reagan) he would emulate most. Both the challenge and political reality of governing among the checks and balances of coequal branches and a federalist system (with state and local powers) shifted that narrative many times during his eight years in office. During his first two years, his party controlled both houses of Congress, and many of Obama's initiatives were passed (including major reforms to America's health care system). Republicans won back the House of Representatives in the midterm elections of 2010, largely due to the emergence of the conservative Tea Party Movement (which supported smaller government, lower taxes, and opposed Obama's health care reform). Despite continuing economic challenges, Obama secured reelection in 2012 by defeating Republican nominee Mitt Romney, but his electoral coattails were short and the House remained in Republican control. The narrative of the Obama years then shifted to one of a lame-duck, second-term president, especially when Republicans won back control of the Senate in 2014. This GOP triumph meant that Obama had little prospect of making any legislative progress on his policy agenda.

While many factors can explain Obama's difficulties in governing, the challenges he encountered stemmed from two major factors. First, for better or worse, the United States government is a two-party system. This is determined mostly by the U.S. Constitution, which provides for single-member districts in the House, and winner-take-all elections for both Congress and the presidency (the latter through the Electoral College). Third or minor parties have little or no chance of gaining traction in the American political system, since even a 20 percent showing in an election nets no representation in the government. While a two-party system may seem less complicated compared to the numerous multiparty parliamentary systems throughout the world, in many ways, it can be even more limiting for governing options. Presidents have fewer opportunities for coalition building on most issues. Often, policy decisions on Capitol Hill are an either-or proposition. From the White House perspective, and to borrow a much-quoted paraphrase from President George W. Bush when speaking about the War on Terror in 2001, you're either "with us or against us."

Second, and perhaps even more important for Obama, is the fact that voter loyalty to a party is not guaranteed. While the Democrats controlled both houses of Congress in 2009, when Obama took the oath of office, they lost both houses during his presidency. While it is not uncommon for a president's party to lose seats in Congress during his time in office, it can make governing more difficult, though occasionally a president (like Bill Clinton) can have success in compromising with the opposing party when it controls Congress.

Now that Obama has been out of office for a few years, many scholars and pundits alike have already attempted to determine his legacy. His party's loss of the presidency to Trump certainly says something about Obama's longer-term effect on the political environment as well as that of the 2016 Democratic nominee (Hillary Clinton). For some, the expectation of the Obama presidency never lived up to the actual results. As with most presidential legacies, it will take decades to fully understand, and all presidents have strengths and weaknesses in this regard. Despite Clinton's loss in 2016, and in defense of Obama (and other presidents who came before him), perhaps it is the American public who need to rethink job performance in the Oval Office. American voters want transformational leadership in their presidents, yet that style of leadership may not be possible in this current political environment. Or, at the very least, it may be much too soon to be thinking of Obama in those terms, despite the early proclamations by some that Obama's time in office would indeed by transformational.

For example, whatever one's views about the merits of the program, passage of the Affordable Care Act in 2010 was a major legislative achievement on a par with Franklin D. Roosevelt's Social Security program in 1935 and Lyndon Johnson's passage of Medicare in 1965. But, while media coverage constantly framed "Obamacare" as a win or a loss for the president based on the most recent statistics about those enrolled, costs rising or falling, etc., it will be years, or perhaps even decades, before any real determination can be made about success or failure of the program. Even the cases that went before the Supreme Court about the policy only highlights the fact that this type of legislative domestic program is a work in progress subject to alterations (both large and small) for many years to come.

Also consider the foreign policy issues that Obama faced. While the wars in Iraq and Afghanistan, begun during the George W. Bush administration, may have technically ended, the battle against ISIS in the Middle East and other terrorist groups around the globe have continued into the Trump administration. Even the agreement reached by the Obama administration with Iran over its nuclear program, which may have been one of the most significant foreign policy achievements of Obama's presidency, was undone by the Trump administration. The swift dismantling of that agreement shows how quickly a signature achievement can disappear when the next occupant of the Oval Office arrives.

The takeaway from these early discussions about Obama's legacy seem to only highlight the fact that transformational leadership, or what some scholars refer to as "presidential greatness," is perhaps impossible in a political environment so dominated by hyper-partisanship. Most of the modern presidents (an era that begins with Franklin D. Roosevelt) had moments of greatness and historic achievements. However, sustaining that greatness, or being consistently transformational during a two-term presidency spanning eight years, is unrealistic. Even having one's party maintain control of both houses of Congress for one term, let alone two, has become a Herculean task. The last president to accomplish the latter was Roosevelt. Elected to an unprecedented (and now impossible due to constitutional term limits) fourth term in 1944 just months before his death, Roosevelt enjoyed Democratic control of both the House and Senate throughout his years in office that accounted for more than 12 years. None of the presidents who have succeeded him have enjoyed such an advantage for the entirety of their presidencies.

If beauty is in the eye of the beholder, so too is presidential greatness, transformational leadership, and presidential legacy. Moreover, today's media-saturated political environment may demand instant gratification and snap judgements. But judging the merits of a president and his time in office should not be rushed. Assessing the true impact and legacy of each president requires an understanding of how their presidencies ultimately fit in the wider arc of American history.

THE CHALLENGE OF GOVERNING

While Obama's presidency offers many valuable lessons, success for future presidents often comes down to the limits of presidential power—or conversely, whether a president can expand the powers of the office. For example, challenges abound regarding the issue of presidential war powers. While Congress, as specified in Article I Section 8 of the U.S. Constitution, has the specific and enumerated power to "declare" war, the president, on the other hand, serves as commander in chief and has the implied power to "make" war. Yet Congress has not officially declared war since December 1941, after the Japanese bombing of Pearl Harbor. Of the more than ten conflicts in which the United States has participated since 1945 (including the Korean War, the Vietnam War, the Persian Gulf War, and the more recent wars in Afghanistan and Iraq), not one was sanctioned by a congressional declaration of war. Instead, all have been initiated by presidents. As many scholars have noted over the years, members of Congress in recent decades became more concerned with reelection than making tough decisions (like declaring war) over which they could lose votes. As a result, they have willingly relinquished the legislature's power to declare war. American presidents, for their part, willingly seized the power not specifically granted to them by the Constitution, thereby enhancing their ability to pursue foreign-policy objectives with few political impediments.

In an attempt to clarify this constitutional ambiguity over war powers, Congress passed the War Powers Resolution (and overrode Richard Nixon's veto of the bill) in 1973. The War Powers Resolution requires the president to consult with Congress prior to engaging troops in military operations, but it also simultaneously recognizes a presidential power to respond to exigent circumstances without notification when such notification would compromise the integrity or effectiveness of the necessary military action. The net effect of this concession was an acknowledgment in all but word of a presidential power to declare war through a statutory loophole. While the constitutionality of the War Powers Resolution remains to be seen more than four decades after its passage—the U.S. Supreme Court has not yet had an opportunity to weigh in on the issue—every president since Jimmy Carter (1977–1981) has relied on this war powers loophole to begin or augment U.S. military action in various parts of the world.

Institutional factors can also limit presidential powers. Depending on one's perspective, this may be a burden on presidents and their ability to get things done or a necessary check against expansive presidential powers. For several decades, for example, Americans have become accustomed to "lame-duck" presidencies during the entire four years of a second term. Despite talk of enduring legacies in the afterglow of a president's reelection victory, the political fortunes of presidents who win reelection often seem to shift dramatically during their second terms. Immediately following his reelection in 2004, George W. Bush proclaimed that voters had given him political capital and he intended to use it. However, 2005 and 2006 turned out to be perhaps his worst years in office. They were marked by plummeting approval ratings in the aftermath of the federal government's ineffective response to Hurricane Katrina's devastation of the U.S. Gulf Coast, the revelation by the *New York Times* of the Bush administration's secret wiretapping program, and diminished public support for the wars in Iraq and Afghanistan. By the end of 2006, and with the help of a few congressional scandals, Bush and the Republicans had lost control of both houses of Congress, which left little opportunity for Bush to accomplish much during his final two years in office.

Bill Clinton didn't fare much better during his second term, though his approval ratings were helped by a period of strong economic growth. Still, despite the promise of productive bipartisanship with the Republican-controlled Congress after reaching a balanced-budget deal in 1997, the next year was dominated by personal scandal that culminated in Clinton's impeachment by the House of Representatives in late 1998. Despite his acquittal by the Senate in early 1999, the momentum for any Clinton policy initiatives had been lost.

While each of the last three second-term presidents has faced unique political circumstances and challenges, many other factors contribute to this trend of political stalemate during a second-term presidency. First, it is common for a president's party to lose congressional seats during midterm elections. This can be particularly problematic for Democrats as Republicans routinely enjoy higher voter turnout in nonpresidential elections (though 2018 was the exception as Democrats won back the House). Second, the American political environment is dominated by a never-ending presidential campaign cycle. Media speculation about who will run, and who might win, in the next presidential election can begin as early as a few weeks before a current campaign even ends. This dynamic can leave many within the political process looking past the current president as they consider how the next election might impact their own political fortunes.

Third, the presidential term limits imposed by the 22nd Amendment to the U.S. Constitution automatically make a second-term president a lame duck. This amendment was first introduced by a Republican-controlled Congress in 1947 as a response to Roosevelt's election to an unprecedented fourth term in 1944. Ratified by the necessary three-fourths of the states in 1951, the amendment's stipulation of a two-term limit for the presidency removes any possibility that a popular president might seek a third term (and thus maintain accountability among the electorate). Of the two-term presidents since the 1950s, only Clinton and Obama might have otherwise considered a third term. The age and declining health of both Dwight Eisenhower and Ronald Reagan would have more than likely prevented each from running again, and George W. Bush's unpopularity by 2008 would have created a major electoral hurdle. For Obama, it was difficult to imagine him *wanting* to run again, but his skill as a candidate, and his relative youth for an outgoing president (55 when he left office in 2017), would have kept the possibility open.

In the final analysis, presidents tend to have their best chance of doing big things during their first two years in office. While many questioned Obama's decision to pursue health care reform during his first year, in hindsight, there was never going to be a better time to accomplish this goal than when he had his highest approval ratings and the largest majority of Democrats in Congress. Presidents and their advisors probably recognize that reality and are best served by a strategy that political scientist James Pfiffner calls "hitting the ground running" when they first take office.

Meanwhile, perhaps Americans should adjust their expectations for a second-term presidency, as the window for major domestic policy change seems to be permanently closed by the tough political environment in which lame-duck presidents operate. Despite the seemingly rational logic that a president who will never again have to face voters can make tough political decisions about important public policies (such as reforming Social Security), members of the president's party in Congress do not have that same luxury.

Foreign policy seems to be the one area in which second-term presidents can still make important and long-lasting decisions, which probably provided little comfort to Obama, who campaigned on a platform to provide broad domestic policy changes. Instead, the last years of his presidency seemed to focus mainly on foreign rather than domestic policy. Yet even in the realm of foreign policy, he devoted much of his focus in his later years in office to international issues that were not among the major policy goals he set at the start of his presidency like ending U.S. involvement in the Middle East.

CONCLUSION

Every four years, those voters who pay close attention to politics become enamored with a presidential candidate. Some voters like to back the candidate who is most viable and has the best odds of winning their party's nomination as well as the presidency. Others set practicality aside and support so-called dark-horse candidates who don't have as much name recognition but who present appealing characteristics or policy prescriptions. Regardless, most American voters (at least when they spend time thinking about it) have an image in their mind of the "perfect" president, on both a personal and political level. However, that "perfect" image is perhaps just an illusion that voters want to find. In reality, the presidency remains one of the most challenging political jobs in the world, and while at times it is perhaps one of the most powerful, it is also limited in many ways. The American presidency has changed in numerous important ways from the somewhat humble office the framers designed, but even after the passage of centuries, the power of the Oval Office remains constrained by the system of checks and balances that the founding fathers designed.

Bibliography

Abraham, Henry J. 2008. *Justices, Presidents, and Senators: A History of U.S. Supreme Court Appointments from Washington to Bush II*, 5th ed. Lanham, MD: Rowman & Littlefield.

Adler, David Gray, and Michael A. Genovese, eds. 2002. *The Presidency and the Law: The Clinton Legacy.* Lawrence, KS: University Press of Kansas.

Adler, David Gray, and Larry N. George, eds. 1996. *The Constitution and the Conduct of American Foreign Policy.* Lawrence, KS: University Press of Kansas.

Ambar, Saladin M. 2016. "Woodrow Wilson." In *The Presidents and the Constitution: A Living History,* ed. Ken Gormley. New York: New York University Press.

Azari, Julia R., Lara M. Brown, and Zim G. Nwokora, eds. 2013. *The Presidential Leadership Dilemma: Between the Constitution and a Political Party.* Albany, NY: SUNY Press.

Barber, James David. 2008. *The Presidential Character: Predicting Performance in the White House,* rev. 4th ed. New York: Prentice Hall.

Barilleaux, Ryan J. 1988. *The Post-Modern Presidency: The Office after Ronald Reagan.* New York: Praeger.

Barilleaux, Ryan J., and Christopher S. Kelley, eds. 2010. *The Unitary Executive and the Modern Presidency.* College Station, TX: Texas A&M University Press.

Baum, Lawrence. 2007. *The Supreme Court,* 9th ed., Washington, DC: CQ Press.

Berger, Raoul. 1973. *Impeachment: The Constitutional Problems.* Cambridge, MA: Harvard University Press.

Berger, Raoul. 1974. *Executive Privilege.* Cambridge, MA: Harvard University Press.

Berman, Larry. 1987. *The New American Presidency.* New York: Little Brown.

Bessette, Joseph, and Jeffrey Tulis. 1981. *The Presidency in the Constitutional Order.* Baton Rouge, LA: Louisiana University Press.

Binder, Sarah A., and Forrest Maltzman. 2009. *Advice and Dissent: The Struggle to Shape the Federal Judiciary.* Washington, DC: Brookings Institution Press.

Bond, Jon, and Richard Fleisher. 1990. *The President in the Legislative Arena.* Chicago, IL: University of Chicago Press.

Borrelli, MaryAnne. 2011. *The Politics of the President's Wife.* College Station, TX: Texas A&M University Press.

Brace, Paul, and Barbara Hinckley. 1992. *Follow the Leader: Opinion Polls and Modern Presidents.* New York: Basic Books.

Buchanan, Bruce. 2013. *Presidential Power and Accountability: Toward a Presidential Accountability System.* New York: Routledge.

Burke, John. 1992. *The Institutional Presidency.* Baltimore, MD: Johns Hopkins University Press.

Cameron, Charles. 2000. *Veto Bargaining: Presidents and the Politics of Negative Power.* New York: Cambridge University Press.

Campbell, Karlyn Kohrs, and Kathleen Hall Jamieson. 1990. *Deeds Done in Words: Presidential Rhetoric and the Genres of Governance.* Chicago, IL: University of Chicago Press.

Canes-Wrone, Brandice. 2006. *Who Leads Whom? Presidents, Policy, and the Public.* Chicago, IL: University of Chicago Press.

Cohen, Jeffrey E. 1997. *Presidential Responsiveness and Public Policy-Making: The Public and the Policies That Presidents Choose.* Ann Arbor, MI: University of Michigan Press.

Cohen, Jeffrey E. 2009. *Going Local: Presidential Leadership in the Post-Broadcast Age.* New York: Cambridge University Press.

Cohen, Jeffrey E., and David Nice. 2003. *The Presidency.* New York: McGraw-Hill.

Conley, Patricia. 2001. *Presidential Mandates: How Elections Shape the National Agenda.* Chicago, IL: Chicago University Press.

Cornwell, Elmer, Jr. 1965. *Presidential Leadership of Public Opinion.* Bloomington, IN: Indiana University Press.

Corwin, Edward S. 1940. *The President: Office and Powers.* New York: New York University Press.

Cronin, Thomas E., and Michael A. Genovese. 1998. *The Paradoxes of the American Presidency.* New York: Oxford University Press.

Dickinson, Matthew J. 1996. *Bitter Harvest: FDR, Presidential Power and the Growth of the Presidential Branch.* Cambridge, MA: Cambridge University Press.

Dolan, Chris J., John Frendreis, and Raymond Tatalovich. 2007. *The Presidency and Economic Policy.* New York: Rowman & Littlefield.

Druckman, James N., and Lawrence R. Jacobs. 2015. *Who Governs? Presidents, Public Opinion, and Manipulation.* Chicago, IL: University of Chicago Press.

Edwards, George C., III. 1989. *At the Margins: Presidential Leadership of Congress.* New Haven, CT: Yale University Press.

Edwards, George C., III. 2003. *On Deaf Ears: The Limits of the Bully Pulpit.* New Haven, CT: Yale University Press.

Edwards, George C., III. 2011. *Why the Electoral College Is Bad for America*, 2nd ed. New Haven, CT: Yale University Press.

Edwards, George C., III. 2012. *Overreach: Leadership in the Obama Presidency.* Princeton, NJ: Princeton University Press.

Edwards, George C. III, and Stephen J. Wayne, eds. 1983. *Studying the Presidency.* Knoxville, TN: University of Tennessee Press.

Eisinger, Robert. 2003. *The Evolution of Presidential Polling.* New York: Cambridge University Press.

Emery, Michael, and Edwin Emery. 1996. *The Press and America: An Interpretive History of the Mass Media*, 8th ed. Boston, MA: Allyn and Bacon.

Eshbaugh-Soha, Matthew, and Jeffrey S. Peake. 2011. *Breaking through the Noise: Presidential Leadership, Public Opinion, and the News Media.* Stanford, CA: Stanford University Press.

Farnsworth, Stephen J. 2009. *Spinner in Chief: How Presidents Sell Their Policies and Themselves.* Boulder, CO: Paradigm Publishers.

Farnsworth, Stephen J. 2018. *Presidential Communication and Character: White House News Management from Clinton and Cable to Twitter and Trump.* New York: Routledge.

Farnsworth, Stephen J., and S. Robert Lichter. 2006. *The Mediated Presidency: Television News and Presidential Governance.* Lanham, MD: Rowman & Littlefield.

Fisher, Louis. 1998. *The Politics of Shared Power: Congress and the Executive*, 4th ed. College Station, TX: Texas A&M University Press.

Fisher, Louis. 2004a. *The Politics of Executive Privilege.* Durham, NC: Carolina Academic Press.

Fisher, Louis. 2004b. *Presidential War Power*, 2nd ed. Lawrence, KS: University Press of Kansas.

Fisher, Louis. 2014. *Constitutional Conflicts between Congress and the President.* Lawrence, KS: University Press of Kansas.

Genovese, Michael A., Todd L. Belt, and William W. Lammers. 2014. *The Presidency and Domestic Policy: Comparing Leadership Styles, FDR to Obama*, 2nd ed. Boulder, CO: Paradigm Publishers.

Goldman, Sheldon. 1997. *Picking Federal Judges: Lower Court Selection from Roosevelt through Reagan.* New Haven, CT: Yale University Press.

Gormley, Ken, ed. 2016. *The Presidents and the Constitution: A Living History*. New York: New York University Press.

Graber, Doris A., and Johanna Dunaway. 2017. *Mass Media and American Politics*, 10th ed. Thousand Oaks, CA: CQ Press.

Greenstein, Fred I. 2009. *The Presidential Difference: Leadership Style from FDR to Barack Obama*, 3rd ed. Princeton, NJ: Princeton University Press.

Hadley, Arthur T. 1976. *The Invisible Primary*. Englewood Cliffs, NJ: Prentice-Hall.

Han, Lori Cox. 2001. *Governing from the Center Stage: White House Communication Strategies during the Television Age of Politics*. Cresskill, NJ: Hampton Press.

Han, Lori Cox. 2015. *In It to Win: Electing Madam President*. New York: Bloomsbury.

Han, Lori Cox, ed. 2018a. *Hatred of America's Presidents: Personal Attacks on the White House from Washington to Trump*. Santa Barbara, CA: ABC-CLIO.

Han, Lori Cox, ed. 2018b. *New Directions in the American Presidency*, 2nd ed. New York: Routledge.

Han, Lori Cox, and Diane J. Heith, eds. 2005. *In the Public Domain: Presidents and the Challenges of Public Leadership*. Albany, NY: SUNY Press.

Hart, Roderick P. 1987. *The Sound of Leadership: Presidential Communication in the Modern Age*. Chicago, IL: University of Chicago Press.

Heith, Diane J. 2004. *Polling to Govern: Public Opinion and Presidential Leadership*. Palo Alto, CA: Stanford University Press.

Heith, Diane J. 2013. *The Presidential Road Show: Public Leadership in an Era of Party Polarization and Media Fragmentation*. Boulder, CO: Paradigm Publishers.

Herring, George C. 2001. *America's Longest War: The United States and Vietnam, 1950–1975*. New York: McGraw-Hill.

Hoffman, Donna, and Alison Howard. 2006. *Addressing the State of the Union: The Evolution and Impact of the President's Big Speech*. Boulder, CO: Lynne Rienner.

Hopper, Jennifer. 2017. *Presidential Framing in the 21st Century News Media: The Politics of the Affordable Care Act*. New York: Routledge.

Howell, William G. 2003. *Power without Persuasion: The Politics of Direct Presidential Action*. Princeton, NJ: Princeton University Press.

Jentleson, Bruce W. 2010. *American Foreign Policy: The Dynamics of Choice in the 21st Century*. New York: W.W. Norton.

Jones, Charles O. 1999. *Separate But Equal Branches: Congress and the Presidency*, 2nd ed. New York: Chatham House Publishers.

Kernell, Samuel. 2007. *Going Public: New Strategies of Presidential Leadership*, 4th ed. Washington, DC: CQ Press.

Kessel, John H. 2001. *Presidents, the Presidency, and the Political Environment*. Washington, DC: CQ Press.

Koenig, Louis W. 1996. *The Chief Executive*, 6th ed. New York: Harcourt Brace.

Kriner, Douglas L. 2010. *After the Rubicon: Congress, Presidents, and the Politics of Waging War*. Chicago, IL: University of Chicago Press.

Kumar, Martha Joynt. 2007. *Managing the President's Message: The White House Communications Operation*. Baltimore, MD: The Johns Hopkins University Press.

Lammers, William W., and Michael A. Genovese. 2000. *The Presidency and Domestic Policy: Comparing Leadership Styles, FDR to Clinton*. Washington, DC: CQ Press.

Laracey, Mel. 2002. *Presidents and the People: The Partisan Story of Going Public*. College Station, TX: Texas A&M University Press.

Leuchtenburg, William. 1963. *Franklin D. Roosevelt and the New Deal: 1932–1940*. New York: Harper and Row.

Levin, Martin A., Daniel DiSalvo, and Martin M. Shapiro, eds. 2012. *Building Coalitions, Making Policy: The Politics of the Clinton, Bush, and Obama Presidencies*. Baltimore, MD: Johns Hopkins University Press.

Lewis, David E. 2008. *The Politics of Presidential Appointments: Political Control and Bureaucratic Performance*. Princeton, NJ: Princeton University Press.

Light, Paul. 1998. *The President's Agenda: Domestic Policy Choice from Kennedy to Clinton*. Baltimore, MD: Johns Hopkins University Press.

Maltese, John Anthony. 1994. *Spin Control: The White House Office of Communications and the Management of Presidential News*, rev. 2nd ed. Chapel Hill, NC: University of North Carolina Press.

Mayer, Kenneth R. 2001. *With the Stroke of a Pen: Executive Orders and Presidential Power*. Princeton, NJ: Princeton University Press.

McKenzie, G. Galvin. 1981. *The Politics of Presidential Appointments*. New York: Free Press.

Milkis, Sidney, and Michael Nelson. 2016. *The American Presidency: Origins and Development 1776–2014*, 7th ed. Washington, DC: CQ Press.

Murray, Robert K., and Tim H. Blessing. 1994. *Greatness in the White House: Rating the Presidents from George Washington Through Ronald Reagan*, 2nd ed. University Park, PA: Pennsylvania State University Press.

Nelson, Michael, and Russell L. Riley, eds. 2011. *Governing at Home: The White House and Domestic Policymaking*. Lawrence, KS: University Press of Kansas.

Neustadt, Richard E. 1990. *Presidential Power and the Modern Presidents: The Politics of Leadership from Roosevelt to Reagan.* New York: Free Press.

O'Brien, David M. 2008. *Storm Center: The Supreme Court in American Politics*, 8th ed. New York: W.W. Norton.

Patterson, Bradley H., Jr. 2000. *The White House Staff: Inside the West Wing and Beyond.* Washington, DC: Brookings Institution Press.

Peterson, Mark A. 1990. *Legislating Together: The White House and Capitol Hill from Eisenhower to Reagan.* Cambridge, MA: Harvard University Press.

Pfiffner, James P. 1996. *The Strategic Presidency: Hitting the Ground Running*, 2nd ed. Lawrence, KS: University Press of Kansas.

Pika, Joseph A., John Anthony Maltese, and Andrew Rudalevige. 2017. *The Politics of the Presidency*, 9th ed. Washington, DC: CQ Press.

Polsby, Nelson W., and Aaron Wildavsky. 2004. *Presidential Elections: Strategies and Structures of American Politics*, 11th ed. Lanham, MD: Rowman & Littlefield.

Polsky, Andrew J. 2012. *Elusive Victories: The American Presidency at War.* New York: Oxford University Press.

Ragsdale, Lyn. 2009. *Vital Statistics on the Presidency: George Washington to George W. Bush*, 3rd ed. Washington, DC: CQ Press.

Rodman, Peter W. 2009. *Presidential Command: Power, Leadership, and the Making of Foreign Policy from Richard Nixon to George W. Bush.* New York: Alfred A. Knopf.

Rose, Richard. 1991. *The Postmodern President*, 2nd ed. Chatham, NJ: Chatham House.

Rossiter, Clinton. 1956. *The American Presidency.* New York: Harcourt, Brace.

Rottinghaus, Brandon. 2010. *The Provisional Pulpit: Modern Presidential Leadership of Public Opinion.* College Station, TX: Texas A&M University Press.

Rozell, Mark. 2000. *Executive Privilege: The Dilemma of Secrecy and Democratic Accountability.* Lawrence, KS: University Press of Kansas.

Rudalevige, Andrew. 2002. *Managing the President's Program: Presidential Leadership and Legislative Policy Formation.* Princeton, NJ: Princeton University Press.

Saunders, Elizabeth N. 2011. *Leaders at War: How Presidents Shape Military Interventions.* Ithaca, NY: Cornell University Press.

Schier, Steven, ed. 2000. *The Postmodern Presidency: Bill Clinton's Legacy in U.S. Politics.* Pittsburgh, PA: University of Pittsburgh Press.

Schlesinger, Arthur M., Jr. 1973. *The Imperial Presidency.* Boston, MA: Houghton Mifflin.

Shull, Steven A. 2000. *American Civil Rights Policy from Truman to Clinton: The Role of Presidential Leadership.* Armonk, NY: M.E. Sharpe.

Silverstein, Mark. 1994. *Judicious Choices: The New Politics of Supreme Court Confirmations*. New York: W.W. Norton.

Sinclair, Barbara. 2007. *Unorthodox Lawmaking: New Legislative Processes in the U.S. Congress*, 3rd ed. Washington DC: CQ Press.

Skowronek, Stephen. 1993. *The Politics Presidents Make: Leadership from John Adams to George Bush*. Cambridge, MA: Belknap/Harvard Press.

Sorenson, Theodore. 2005. *Decision Making in the White House: The Olive Branch or the Arrows*. New York: Columbia University Press.

Spanier, John, and Steven W. Hook. 2009. *American Foreign Policy since World War II*. Washington, DC: CQ Press.

Stuckey, Mary E. 1991. *The President as Interpreter-in-Chief*. Chatham, NJ: Chatham House.

Sullivan, Terry, ed. 2004. *The Nerve Center: Lessons in Governing from the White House Chiefs of Staff*. College Station, TX: Texas A&M University Press.

Tebbel, John, and Sarah Miles Watts. 1985. *The Press and the Presidency: From George Washington to Ronald Reagan*. New York: Oxford University Press.

Tulis, Jeffrey K. 1987. *The Rhetorical Presidency*. Princeton, NJ: Princeton University Press.

Warber, Adam. 2006. *Executive Orders and the Modern Presidency*. Boulder, CO: Lynne Rienner.

Warshaw, Shirley Anne. 2000. *The Keys to Power: Managing the Presidency*. New York: Longman.

Watson, Robert P. 2000. *The President's Wives: Reassessing the Office of First Lady*. Boulder, CO: Lynne Rienner.

Wattenberg, Martin J. 1991. *The Rise of Candidate-Centered Politics: Presidential Elections of the 1980s*. Cambridge, MA: Harvard University Press.

Weko, Thomas J. 1995. *The Politicizing Presidency: The White House Personnel Office, 1948–1994*. Lawrence, KS: University of Kansas Press.

Wildavsky, Aaron. 1966. "The Two Presidencies." *Trans-Action* 4(2), 7–14.

Yalof, David Alistair. 1999. *Pursuit of Justices: Presidential Politics and the Selection of Supreme Court Nominees*. Chicago, IL: University of Chicago Press.

Index

About the Author

Lori Cox Han is a professor of political science at Chapman University. Her research and teaching expertise include the presidency, women and politics, media and politics, and political leadership. She has authored and coauthored numerous books, including *Advising Nixon: The White House Memos of Patrick J. Buchanan* (2019); *Presidents and the American Presidency*, 2nd ed. (2018); *Women, Power, and Politics: The Fight for Gender Equality in the United States* (2018); *In It to Win: Electing Madam President* (2015); and *A Presidency Upstaged: The Public Leadership of George H. W. Bush* (2011). She is also the editor of several scholarly volumes, including *Madam President? Gender and Politics on the Road to the White House* (2020); *Hatred of America's Presidents: Personal Attacks on the White House from Washington to Trump* (ABC-CLIO, 2018); and *New Directions in the American Presidency*, 2nd ed. (2018). Her research has been published in *PS: Political Science & Politics, American Politics Research, Presidential Studies Quarterly,* and *Congress and the Presidency*. Dr. Han is the former president of Presidents and Executive Politics, an organized section of the American Political Science Association devoted to the study of the presidency.

૧|૨